QUALITATIVE ENQUIRY FOR RURAL DEVELOPMENT

A Review

Jon Moris and
James Copestake

INTERMEDIATE TECHNOLOGY PUBLICATIONS
on behalf of the
OVERSEAS DEVELOPMENT INSTITUTE
1993

Intermediate Technology Publications Ltd
103-105 Southampton Row, London WC1B 4HH, UK

© Overseas Development Institute 1993

A CIP record for this book is available from the British Library

ISBN 1 85339 215 4

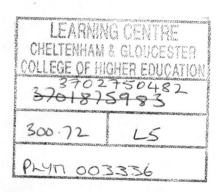
Typesetting by ODI and Inforum Typesetting, Rowlands Castle, Hants
Printed by BPCC, Exeter

Contents

1 Introduction   1

   1.1   Outline   1
   1.2   Definition of qualitative enquiry   3

2 The Need for Qualitative Enquiry   9

   2.1   Institutional context   9
   2.2   Spheres of activity   12
   2.3   Key tasks   15
       Planning   16
       Implementation   18
       Evaluation   23
   2.4   Some neglected variables   25
       At the agency level   25
       At the community level   30
   2.5   Criteria for effective information supply   34

3 The Nature of Qualitative Enquiry   36

   3.1   A rapid literature review   36
       Social science research   36
       Rapid rural appraisal (RRA)   38
       Evaluation of social development projects   40
       Policy analysis   44
       Parallel developments in quantitative enquiry   45
   3.2   Some unifying principles   45
       Methodological pluralism   46
       Triangulation   47
       Professionalism   51
   3.3   Sources of information   54
       Documents   54
       Field visits   55
       Key informants   58
       Group meetings   59
       Participant observation   60
       Team studies   61
       Action research   62
   3.4   Conclusions: some key concepts   63
       Intelligence rather than applied research   63

Indicators rather than coefficients 63
Key informants rather than respondents 65

4 The Application of Qualitative Enquiry 67

4.1 Agricultural research and technology development 67
    The transfer of technology model 68
    Farming systems research 69
    Farmer participatory research 73
4.2 Other spheres of activity 74
    The project cycle 74
    Planning investments in infrastructure 77
    Public sector services 78
    Marketing 80
    Savings and credit programmes 82
    Disaster response 84
    Sensitive topics 84
    Turbulent conditions 87
4.3 Opportunities and constraints 87
    Methodological weaknesses and research 88
    Ignorance and training 89
    Bureaucracy and institutional reform 90

5 The Future of Qualitative Enquiry 93

5.1 Contemporary trends 93
5.2 Future directions 95
    Real-time surveys 95
    Specialized PRA/RRA 95
    Disaster Response 96
    Bureaucratization of NGO/PVO activities 97
5.3 Conclusion 97

References 99

Index 111

Tables

1	Differences between qualitative and quantitative research	5
2	Socio-economic variables at community and farm levels	11
3	Examples of information needs within different spheres of activity	13
4	Key tasks in the project cycle	15
5	A checklist of neglected variables at the agency level	27
6	Fieldwork strategies	37
7	Indicators for the evaluation of participation	43
8	A logical framework matrix	76
9	Some basic monitoring information needs for rural health, education and extension services	79
10	Checklist of marketing intervention needs	81
11	Data requirements for rapid food security assessment	85

Figure

1	Information flows within a simple model of a rural development agency	10

Boxes

1	'Credit T&V' – a case of a solution in search of a problem?	17
2	Identifying all the stakeholders	19
3	Monitoring cattle dips for the Maasai	22
4	Triangulation in Upper Embu District, Kenya	48
5	Three weeks for preparation of a questionnaire?	50
6	Checking the meaning of quantitative questions	51
7	Uncovering bad data	52
8	The formality of informal visits	56
9	The yam grower	59
10	Deciding when a drought has begun	65
11	Orthodox agricultural research – validating hunches	72
12	Where have all the farmers gone?	77
13	The much-maligned coffee roasters of Bolivia	82
14	The smell of corruption?	86
15	Participatory wealth ranking in Zambia	89
16	A little test	92

Acknowledgements

The origin of this book can be traced back to a workshop organized by Malcolm Hall of FAO in the Autumn of 1989 on the use of different methods of enquiry for agricultural policymaking. Although no published proceedings resulted, the paper prepared by Jon Moris was the kernel from which the book grew. John Farrington at the Overseas Development Institute in London was then instrumental in taking up the suggestion that it might be worked on further. James Copestake completely reformulated and revised the ideas during 1992, and a final text was agreed, after much trans-Atlantic correspondence, during 1993. We wish to thank Malcolm Hall and John Farrington in particular for their help in bringing the book into existence, as well as the Nuffield Foundation for financial support during its reformulation.

As always, many other people provided behind the scenes support. The ODI library staff, especially Peter Ferguson, were untiring in their pursuit of references; and John Farrington, Douglas Horton, Mick Howes, Robert Chambers, Stephen Biggs, Michael Cernea, Mike Collinson, Brian Pratt, Anthony Bebbington and Mike Edwards all made useful contributions to the literature trawl. Michelle Hunsicker in Utah and Alison Saxby at ODI provided vital and unstinting word processing assistance. Nonetheless, we remain jointly responsible for whatever errors and omissions remain in our treatment of this rapidly expanding topic.

1 Introduction

1.1 Outline

THIS BOOK is directed towards individuals engaged in formulating and implementing policies, plans, programmes and projects affecting rural areas of poor countries. For want of a better term, we shall refer to this group as practitioners of rural development. While their precise information requirements are diverse, they all depend in some way upon the systematic collection of information about the households and communities they serve, and the environments in which their clients live and work.

Recognition of the contribution that qualitative enquiry can make and the range of available literature on qualitative techniques have both increased significantly during the last decade. The much recommended text on data collection by Casley and Lury (1981), for example, included two cursory paragraphs on 'quick and dirty' techniques, whereas almost half of the World Bank publication that superseded it (Casley and Kumar, 1988) is concerned with qualitative methods. However, a succinct and non-technical introduction to when and why qualitative techniques of enquiry should be favoured has been lacking. This is what we have set out to provide.

The guide is divided into five parts and can be quickly summarized. In Section 1.2 of Part One we describe what we mean in this context by *qualitative*. Qualitative information is generally thought of as subjective, verbal and descriptive; in contrast to *quantitative* information which is objective, numerical, and amenable to mathematical analysis. On closer examination, however, it can be seen that much numerical data is also qualitative in the first instance – a collection of subjective yes/no answers collected through a survey, for example. We argue that the distinction between quantitative and qualitative enquiry hinges less on the source of information than on the point at which information is codified, or otherwise simplified. Early codification permits rigorous statistical analysis, but at the same time entails introducing restrictive assumptions which limit the range of possible findings. It is a short step from this

1

distinction to the conclusion that qualitative and quantitative methods of enquiry are complementary. We shall argue that the most appropriate blend of the two depends upon the nature of available information and the task at hand.

Part Two provides an overview of the diverse activities carried out by practitioners of rural development, and their respective information requirements. These can be classified in at least three different ways.

1. Section 2.1 discusses the different levels of actors in rural development, and the link between information needs and organizational structure;

2. Section 2.2 lists some of the important spheres of activity that practitioners of rural development engage in: *ad hoc* projects; investment in infrastructure; provision of social and technical services; agricultural research; marketing; banking; disaster response; and natural resource management.

3. Section 2.3 considers the distinction between the evaluation of past actions, monitoring of ongoing actions, and planning of future actions.

The need to complement quantitative methods of data collection with qualitative enquiry emerges clearly in each case.

Part Three starts with a rapid review of three important strands of the literature. The longest and broadest of these is concerned with qualitative research methodology in the social sciences. Rapid Rural Appraisal (RRA) draws extensively upon this tradition, but has grown more directly out of the practical problem of identifying priority areas for action with limited time and resources. More recently, however, its focus has shifted to the issue of participation (by villagers, farmers and other clients of development agencies) and RRA has given way to the acronym PRA or Participatory Rural Appraisal. This is leading to convergence with two additional strands in the literature; one is concerned with participation in rural development that has been derived from the practical experience of private voluntary or non-government organizations (NGOs); and the other is concerned with detailed analysis of policy and the policy process.

Sections 3.3 draws three key unifying principles out of this literature. If equally valid versions of the same reality may be arrived at by different methodologies, practitioners should recognize the value of using more than one method of enquiry (triangulation), and the need to tailor methods of enquiry to specific purposes. Such pluralism is not, however, a licence for haphazard or casual research. Qualitative enquiry is at least as professionally demanding as quantitative enquiry. Section 3.3 then discusses issues and problems that may arise in conducting qualitative enquiry based on different primary sources of information. The trial section concludes by emphasizing the greater appropriateness of: (a) intelligence gathering over formal applied research; (b) indicators over formal estimates of coefficients; (c) key informants over a representative sample of respondents.

Part Four considers the scope for improved applications of qualitative enquiry. Section 4.1 focuses in depth on its application to agricultural research and technology development. While it is in this sphere that some of the most serious efforts have been made to institutionalize qualitative enquiry (as farming systems research), its role and status is still not yet fully secure. Section 4.2 then provides a rapid review of possible applications of qualitative enquiry to each of the spheres of rural development listed in Section 2.2. Section 4.3 concludes by considering obstacles – conceptual, individual and institutional – to qualitative enquiry, and the scope for overcoming them through research, training and reform.

Finally, Part Five considers the future of qualitative enquiry, given contemporary trends in data handling technologies and changing demands for better information.

It is worth making explicit two things that this guide does *not* set out to do. Firstly, it is not intended to be a manual or cookbook of alternative techniques of qualitative enquiry, though it does provide pointers to where such information can be found. Secondly, our primary concern is how the art of collecting data necessary to inform rural development practice can be improved, taking into account existing organizational and resource constraints. Our coverage of the underlying philosophical or epistemological issues, and the extensive literature on qualitative methodology within social science is therefore very limited. Those interested in these deeper issues could start with Patton (1990), Lancy (1993), LeCompte, Millroy, and Preissle (1992), Streiffeler (1990), or Glaser and Strauss (1967); and there are numerous other texts (see bibliography).

1.2 Definition of qualitative enquiry

The distinction between qualitative and quantitative approaches to rural data tends to be drawn as a sharp dichotomy (Cohen, 1973). On the qualitative side, we find anthropologists and historians. Their approaches in the past entailed becoming immersed in primary data (either in documents or through participant observation and extended interviews), before the investigator formulated an inductively derived picture of a specific situation, institution or system. On the quantitative side are agricultural economists, demographers and census-takers whose main interest has been to obtain empirical measurements (either directly or indirectly) which could be analysed within the framework of a

3

deductively justified methodology. At the two extremes, these approaches are very different, as Table 1 illustrates.

Problems arise almost immediately when one tries to put this distinction into practice. For example, throughout this paper the reader will note that we sometimes refer to qualitative sources, sometimes to qualitative data, and sometimes to qualitative methods or techniques. These differences arise because observational data go through several stages in the process of utilization, and quantification can occur at different points in the process. Thus almost any qualitative information can be transformed and treated quantitatively at a higher level of analysis – if only to count the presence or absence of some trait. Indeed, there are well developed statistical rules to govern such transformations (Haberman, 1978).

Similarly, much quantitative data occurs initially as a qualitative report of some activity or observed trait. The initial observations are then converted (reduced) into approximate numeric values for ease of comparison and processing. Much of the original (qualitative) information is lost in this translation, as made clear when it is re-analysed in another way to yield additional insights. For example, the range scientist's aerial photograph can be interpreted qualitatively, by direct inspection, or quantitatively by measuring areas on the photograph that correspond to some system of land-use or vegetation classification.

Perhaps the key difference implied by the distinction between qualitative and quantitative methods is that in the latter case the transformation of the data into numeric form occurs early in the process of information handling, so that the analysis itself can proceed according to statistical rules. Subsequent interpretation is severely constrained by the assumptions employed in the initial reduction of data to numeric form, and depends heavily upon the mathematical rules governing how such information can be treated and interpreted.

Further clarification concerning the main differences between quantitative and qualitative enquiry emerges if we focus more carefully on how data are collected. A passive approach to acquiring data occurs through experience, either observing events directly or listening to others as they talk about them. Such observational evidence is clearly qualitative and the only active aspect occurs in regard to how it is recorded.

Still qualitative but more interventionist is the direct questioning of respondents, so that the content of materials recorded has been guided by the investigator. Documentation of responses may take the form of a checklist or questionnaire, further narrowing how responses are treated.

The critical transition into quantitative enquiry occurs when measurement is introduced into the data collection or recording process. It can occur by direct measurement while making field observations or by direct measurements (including rankings) within structured questioning.

4

Table 1: Differences between qualitative and quantitative research

Qualitative		Quantitative	
Captures 'reality' by	Main traits	Captures 'reality' by	Main traits
extended interviews	inductive	physical counts	deductive
photographs and maps, imagery case studies open questions	sampling by value of informant/ document	closed questions	sampling by a pre-determined statistical design
reported happenings	observation recorded in representational form (images, narratives, notes)	reported rates and frequencies	observations recorded as categories or numbers, pre-classified
in-place observation	analysis: free-form to suit investigator isomorphic to context	employs derived quantities: yields, prices, etc.	analysis: closed-form to meet methodological criteria isomorphic to selected variables
reported meanings major intuitive effort by interpreter	situationally driven	major procedural effort by data-handling team	procedurally driven
	sees itself as representing systemic values and specific situations		sees itself as deriving objective facts, adding to general knowledge
	difficult to generalize		easy to generalize

In natural science, much data is recorded in numeric form yielding evidence which experimental scientists consider more objective, and hence, more replicable than other forms of enquiry. A well-prepared socio-economic survey will be designed to elicit easily quantified information from respondents, often through 'closed' rather than open-ended questioning. Such measurement at source is the least ambiguous, but also the most intrusive – we have all experienced the frustration of being required to give a yes/no response to a question, when we really want to reply 'yes, but!'

A study may also become quantitative through the transformation of documented information into numerical form. Such applications of quantified enquiry are essentially non-reactive to the original environment, but still require an extra step which may introduce bias or questionable selectivity.

Whether recorded information is then analysed qualitatively (by direct inference) or quantitatively (by mathematical analysis) introduces a further complication. Policy-makers often make qualitative use of statistical evidence, for example. In the narrowest sense, a fully quantitative study is one where the mathematical processing of the data dictates what is learned. It is, then, more rigorous but also more limited in the use it makes of the original information.

The theoretical issue underlying this paper is whether in rural development we gain from not quantifying information, at least not in the initial stages when it is being acquired and processed. In operational terms, important questions that arise are:

o Is rural information of a form and nature where it retains significant value beyond what would be available when reduced to numeric form according to presently understood conventions?
o Do we find problems in the assumptions which must be made while converting rural information into numeric values?
o Do those who are likely to perform data reduction have the special skills and competency required?
o Can procedurally-driven analysis according to existing quantitative conventions provide all the information required?

On all four counts, we argue that rural data presently obtainable in developing countries is more likely to merit qualitative than quantitative treatment. First, there is often considerable unexploited value in the information itself (depending, of course, on how the information is initially represented). Second, there are many problems associated with the strong assumptions embedded in specific approaches to quantification. Data that are immediately quantified at source are essentially brittle; a change in theoretical and methodological assumptions may invalidate the usefulness of the entire data set. Third, the institutional capacity for generating, analysing and correctly interpreting quantitative data may be weak – although qualitative method (as we shall see) may also stretch individual and institutional capacities. And finally, there are various other approaches which potentially transcend the limitations inherent in much quantitative analysis. This is not to argue that qualitative approaches should be the only ones applied to rural data, but rather to state that they

6

are fully legitimate and sometimes more appropriate than the quantitative alternatives.

While the distinction between quantitative and qualitative is the most important way of illuminating the meaning of qualitative, it also needs to be distinguished clearly from any form of informal or casual enquiry. The distinction does not rest on the source of data, nor even on the way in which the serious investigator is perceived by those he meets, who may indeed find him or her superficially less formal and more relaxed than most officials. Instead, the distinction arises from the fact that good qualitative enquiry is systematic, planned and documented.

Note, however, that this distinction has not always been clearly drawn in the literature. For example the formal/informal terminology has been widely used in papers on farming systems research to mean what we prefer to refer to as the quantitative/qualitative distinction (e.g. Biggs, 1983; Franzel and Crawford, 1987).

Very few practitioners receive training in how to carry out what we can now refer to as formal qualitative enquiry. Instead, most rely upon their own immediate experience, upon reports from their own home communities, and upon chance information from their colleagues. Such sources are naturally of greatly varying relevance and reliability, and their value is diminished by the unselective and uncritical way the information is used. We face the paradox that qualitative sources are probably the most widely used form of information for rural policymaking, but also the most misused. The intrinsic advantage of qualitative enquiry – its comprehensiveness, timeliness and cost-effectiveness – are lost when qualitative sources are employed casually without any awareness of their limitations.

Finally, it is also worth making two further clarifications of our use of the term qualitative. Firstly, it should now be apparent that qualitative should not be confused with quality (i.e. merit). For although qualitative data (derived from extended interviews, for example) may be considered more accurate and reliable than quantitative data (derived from a larger number of more superficial interviews, for example), it is also possible to have 'poor quality' qualitative information, and 'good quality' quantitative information. For variables which can be readily quantified – years of schooling completed, for example – the investigator would be foolish to resort to purely qualitative representation.

Furthermore, so called qualitative indicators may or may not be derived from qualitative enquiry. We can give two examples of this.

O Some sociologists use the phrase qualitative indicators for such variables as access, participation, empowerment, self-reliance and awareness, which are difficult to quantify, but are of critical importance to the promotion of self-sustaining or sustainable

7

development (see Section 3.1). However, qualitative enquiry, as we use it, may be concerned with a far wider range of variables, including those which can in principle also be measured. For example, qualitative enquiry may provide an estimate of crop yields, which can then be cross-checked against estimates based on precise measurement.

○ Some United Nations publications also use the phrase qualitative indicators interchangeably with social indicators, to refer to non-economic indicators of human welfare such as mortality, morbidity and literacy rates (for example UNRISD, 1991). Since most of these statistics are based upon quantitative surveys, we would actually refer to them as quantitative.

2 The Need for Qualitative Enquiry

HAVING STATED that our interest in qualitative enquiry is rooted in the question of how the practice of rural development can be made more effective, it is logical to start by reviewing the diversity of those activities, information needs stemming from them, and what criteria should be applied in evaluating different approaches to obtaining that information. Sections 2.1 to 2.3 consider practitioners' information needs in relation to:

○ institutional context;
○ specific spheres of activity;
○ functional tasks.

Section 2.4 then identifies two particular sets of variables that systematic rural enquiry often neglects, and Section 2.5 concludes the section with a checklist of criteria for the evaluation of different methods of rural enquiry.

2.1 Institutional context

The information requirements of each practitioner of rural development obviously depends upon their role within a given organization, being one component of the larger information system required to meet the organization's goals. Thus it is impossible to consider the efficiency with which practitioners obtain and utilize information without simultaneously considering the institutional structure within which they operate – a point that will become particularly apparent when we discuss participatory forms of rural enquiry in Section 3.1. For example, within most public service departments (such as health, animal husbandry, education or agriculture) at least four decisionmaking levels can be distinguished, with information giving and receiving occurring between them (see Figure 1).

Information as a product arises at every level and can move in either direction. It can also jump upwards directly between non-adjacent categories. A large farm management survey, for example, can transfer

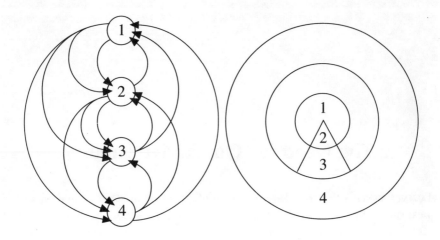

KEY:
1. Policy/macro environment
2. Senior administrators/managers and policymakers
3. Middle/local-level managers, technical and field staff
4. Individuals and households (villagers, farmers, clients,
     community leaders etc. and their environment)

Figure 1:   *Information flows within a simple model of a rural development agency*

information from (4) to (2), without junior staff being privy to the official findings – even if they were responsible for much of the field work. On the other hand, it is far more difficult to miss out levels in disseminating information from the centre to the periphery, other than on a highly selective basis, although radio and other mass media make it relatively easy for those at the centre to pass information to all outer groups simultaneously. Table 2 provides a checklist of some of the information that decisionmakers might need to draw upon at the community and household levels.

Given the complexity of the rural situation in any locality, all mechanisms for collection and absorption of information must be selective. The more intermediaries through which information passes moving up the hierarchy, for example, the more it is likely to be modified – hence the attraction of direct channels of enquiry for those in senior positions. The greater the formal responsibility of persons within an organization, the greater the problem of how to reconcile their information absorption capacity with the total stock of potentially relevant information.

We can identify various strategies that people employ to do this. For example, reliance on aggregate statistical data based on sample surveys may be seen as a mechanism for regulation of information flow from

Table 2:   Socio-economic variables at community and farm levels

Community-level variation

Distribution of holdings by land type
Existing services, rates of growth
Size and characteristics of service centres
Adequacy of communications
Availability of water, power, fuel
Settlement pattern: homesteads vs village
Degree of out-migration, backwash effects
Volume of cash-flow within the local system
Input delivery in place and working?
Nature and strength of local leadership
Degree of communal co-operation
Nature and importance of communal celebrations, events, rituals
Past performance of local projects
Degree of alienation of different groups
How widely are rewards distributed?
Attention or assistance from higher levels? (patron-client ties to 'big men')
Degree of conflict, factionalism
Degree women participate in communal affairs, leadership
Ethnic homo/heterogeneity
Wealth and resources distribution
Demographic characteristics
Attitudinal and prestige systems
Administrative staff characteristics
General incidence of diseases
General levels of security

Farm-level variation

Ownership status; no. of holdings, fields, units
On-farm resource availabilities; size, zone
Quality of land and special characteristics
Farm water supply: adequacy, reliability, distance
Farm energy supplies: nature, adequacy, reliability
Transport and communications situation, remoteness
General climate, on-farm micro-climates
Mix of non-farm enterprises, size and requirements of each
Types of livestock enterprises, degree integration
Quality of husbandry evidenced on major enterprises

Degrees of risk for major enterprises
Innovativeness of the farmer
Degree of farm unification: physical, operational and financial
Monetization of farming practices
On-farm investments: equipment, structure, housing
Household characteristics: size, age and sex, no. of spouses
Household welfare load: aged, inform, alcoholics, young
Household type (single parent, stage in development cycle etc.)
Household labour resources and allocation
Education and experience of farmers and spouse(s)
Degree of extension contact to farm/households
Participation in community: leadership, groups, services
Degree of media use
Farmer's levels of knowledge
Farmer's income/property level (estimated)
Expenditure pattern (farming, household,consumption)
Social status, access to support
Degree of indebtedness

Source: Adapted from Moris (1981:39)

---

source that ensures wide coverage and representativeness. But it is highly selective, expensive and often too slow to keep up with the pace of decisionmaking demands. Decentralization or delegation of decisions, on the other hand, may be seen as a mechanism for managing information by introducing another information filter into the hierarchy. The drawback for many senior decisionmakers is that it may result in reduced control and power within the organization.

In general, most rural agencies are probably so structured (whether by accident or design) that key figures at the centre are left with either too much of the wrong information, or more information of unknown quality than they have time to sift through, and therefore fall back on a mixture of their own past experience, informal data-grabbing exercises and intuition (see Mintzberg, 1973). The issue is then how to acknowledge this fact and find ways of strengthening the effective channels of information, rather than wasting time refining official but unused channels.

2.2 Spheres of activity

Table 3 lists eight spheres of activity, each of which is likely to be associated with its own decisionmaking structure and forms a part of the overall public administration of rural development. There is no particular

Table 3:   Examples of information needs within different spheres of activity

Sphere	Tasks	Events generating extra data needs
Agricultural research and technology development	• Identification of farm constraints • Choice and screening of technology • Identification of recommendation domains • Validation of recommendations	• Expansion into new areas and crops • Pressure on existing farming systems • Changing market conditions • Climate change
Ad hoc projects	• Identification of target groups • Needs assessment • Appraisal • Monitoring • Evaluation	• Unforeseen changes in the project environment • Changing demands and expectations of target group
Public investment in infrastructure	• Planning, co-ordination • Consultation • Design	• Approval of new projects • Cost over-runs, budget cut-backs
Public sector services e.g. agricultural extension, health, education	• Identification of target groups • Choice of technology • Personnel management • Policy formulation	• Annual reviews • Expansion into new areas • Administrative reforms • Donor funding • Budgetary cut-backs

Rural marketing	• Identification of bottlenecks • Formulation and implementation of price and tax policy • Price monitoring	• Seasonal and unexpected changes in supply and demand
Rural banking	• Loan appraisal • Deposit mobilization • Loan recovery • Formulation of interest rate and other levelling policies • Positive 'housekeeping'	• Rescheduling due to drought etc. • Changes in policy • Expansion into new areas and activities
Disaster response	• Positive natural resource monitoring • Early warning systems • Food security assessments	• Crises in food supply or entitlements requiring relief • Military conflict

theoretical rationale underlying this categorization, and other analysts would very likely come up with a different list. It nevertheless highlights the enormous range of topics on which information is required, as well as the breadth of agency activity that practitioners need to keep up to date with.

Given the range of routine activities that each agency has to carry out, any commitment to acquiring additional data in a systematic fashion tends to have a high opportunity cost. The same staff will be in charge of supervising field cadres, of accounting for funds spent, of preparing budgetary estimates, of planning staff work programmes, and of offering any on-the-job training given by the organization. Those at a distance in headquarters often ignore the limited capacity of their own field units, and generate a stream of requests for additional information related to field project and current achievements. Thus, any new request for information is unlikely to be heeded unless it is given a very high priority or requires relatively little extra work. New approaches to rural enquiry – whether qualitative or quantitative – should ideally entail little extra financial outlay, build upon existing reporting systems and not take up too much staff time.

2.3 Key tasks

The information needs of rural development practitioners can also be classified into three broad functional areas, according to whether they are: (a) forward looking, (b) concerned with ongoing activities, or (c) backward looking. Qualitative enquiry can be useful in all three areas. Within the project cycle framework, for example, Table 4 illustrates how it may complement rather than compete with the elaboration of formal analytical methods and decisionmaking procedures.

Table 4:   Key tasks in the project cycle

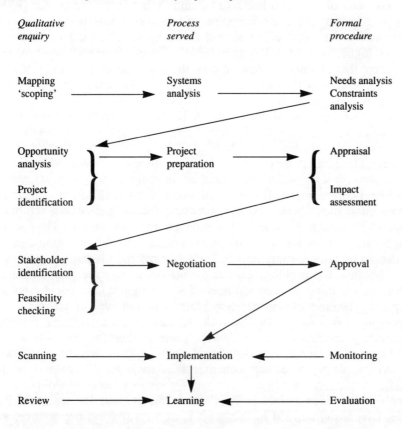

Qualitative enquiry	Process served	Formal procedure
Mapping 'scoping'	Systems analysis	Needs analysis Constraints analysis
Opportunity analysis Project identification	Project preparation	Appraisal Impact assessment
Stakeholder identification Feasibility checking	Negotiation	Approval
Scanning	Implementation	Monitoring
Review	Learning	Evaluation

15

Planning

Forward looking activities include project identification, appraisal and planning in general. Much of it is highly formalized and mechanical, particularly for ongoing activities in stable environments. There are also strong quantitative aspects to appraisal and planning, based on financial information and key physical parameters, such as average crop yields. However, the first steps in identification of a project, or elaboration of a plan are far more difficult to systematize and less amenable to quantitative enquiry. This may be referred to as diagnosis, since it often involves the identification of a problem or constraint. All too often 'solutions' come first and 'problems' are then generated to justify them, while rural people themselves are ignored until interventions have already been launched (see Box 1). More generally, preoccupation with a specific problem, or obsession with a proposed solution, gets in the way of a conscious examination of the more general question of whether problem and proposed solution were reliably identified in the first place.

The term diagnosis is borrowed from farming systems research (FSR), where it refers to the identification of key constraints within a farming system that research effort should focus upon. The goal of screening technologies to suit local systems which is implicit in FSR soon made it apparent that diagnosing what to do – the initial definition of options and of arguments why they are needed – is crucial. For example, agricultural research has generally focused on yields per hectare as the primary criterion of agricultural performance. However, returns per unit of land matter only when land has become a key limiting factor on production, and farming systems researchers quickly established that this is not always the case. It may be true for most irrigated rice production, for example, (though water may also be limiting), or in densely settled highland communities. However, in much of tropical Africa farmers are more concerned about riskiness, breaking the hunger period, returns to labour at critical periods and avoidance of cash inputs. Thus at the diagnostic phase we want to make certain we do not prejudge the outcome by prior assumptions built into formalized planning procedures.

The case for probing, careful qualitative analysis at the diagnostic stage of planning is even stronger if we recognize that constraints are typically layered on top of each other; that removal of an immediate constraint often simply brings to the surface an underlying but invisible secondary constraint (Moris, 1981). There is therefore an unavoidable element of judgement in deciding how to allocate resources towards activities aimed at easing constraints at each level. Table 4 adopts Keller's suggestion (1990) that we distinguish between 'opportunity analysis' and 'constraints analysis' when carrying out diagnosis (see Box 11). Diagnosis, defined in this way, is clearly of wide importance, and may emerge from prior monitoring and evaluation work rather than be

Box 1:   'Credit T&V' – A case of a solution in search of a problem?

The 'training and visit' system has been adopted, with World Bank support, by many countries.   Its essence is to improve communication between farmers, agricultural extension workers, and more senior extension staff through adherence to a carefully monitored routine of visits.   Without entering into a discussion of how successful the T&V has been, we may note that it proved a successful formula for packaging World Bank aid to the agricultural sector.

In India, from 1970 onwards, the World Bank also channelled a considerable amount of funding into agriculture through the rural banking system (Copestake, 1988).   However, World Bank officials became increasingly concerned about the financial health of rural banking, as measured both by loan repayment rates and bank profitability.   Continued external finance was therefore made conditional upon a series of measures specifically designed to improve loan recovery.   One of these was the 'pilot project to strengthen the credit delivery system'.

This pilot project was widely referred to by Indian bankers as 'Credit T&V' because, it sought to regularize contacts between farmers and bank staff, as T&V had set out to do in agricultural extension.

When I was assigned to assist in developing the methodology for evaluation of the pilot project, I first asked for project design documents, so that I could study the original goals and thinking behind the project.   Nobody could provide them, and important differences of view emerged about what the rationale of the project actually was.   Some saw it as a strictly financial experiment – would the costs of extra expenditure on loan supervision be outweighed by improved repayment?   Others argued that as credit was subsidized, it was right and natural that credit supervision should also be subsidized.   What became clear, was that the design of the project was based on a blueprint lifted from another context, rather than a careful process of consultation and analysis of the causes of poor loan recovery in India.

procedurally separate from it (Casley and Kumar, 1987).

In all cases, however, the key task is to identify constraints and opportunities; both immediate and hidden, and at all levels of decisionmaking. The early coding of responses implicit in quantitative enquiry means that it is generally a weak tool for diagnosis, since the whole point is to identify which assumptions are valid, and hence which more structured modes of analysis can be applied usefully. For example, it is useful to explore perceived problems and options, as well as proposed solutions of different actors (with supporting arguments), and to identify dimensions and aspects which can be eliminated from further enquiry. It is also important to scan across all relevant aspects of the environment and its constituent systems; and if it is possible to build up a structural picture of how the various sub-components are interrelated, all the better. Whether they recognize it or not, analysts, when identifying interventions, are necessarily operating on the basis of preconceptions of a wider institutional environment. If this system is in all or part only poorly described, they may need to carry out a substantial amount of institutional 'mapping' to delineate its components and their interlinkages (see Chapter 7 in White, 1990).

These are ambitious goals for any preliminary investigation operating with limited time and resources. The case for using qualitative enquiry in diagnosis is precisely this – that it yields a far higher return (when properly employed) per unit of effort and is more suited to examining a wide range of incommensurate, systematic factors than are the quantitative alternatives. What is lost in certainty and in power of measurement, is gained in speed and breadth.

Rapid Rural Appraisal, which we discuss in Section 3.1, provides an array of methods suited to the 'targeting' process leading into development intervention. In place of an elaborate sequence of required diagnostic procedures (in an irrigation reconnaissance survey examined by one of us 38 separate investigative steps were specified), the investigator, using RRA, is expected to match the techniques to the requirements of the situation (here see Molnar, 1989 and Cernea, 1990).

The transition from planning into implementation occurs when negotiation has been successful (the function served) and approval gained (the procedure completed). Here, too, there is a tendency to think only about necessary procedural inputs: who must sign what documents. Implicit is the assumption that everybody with a vital interest has been consulted (see Box 2). Leaving key players out of relevant negotiations happens frequently, giving those overlooked no incentive to co-operate. We suggest, therefore, that a qualitative assessment of the interests of all players needs to precede opening formal negotiations. It need not be elaborate (assuming analysts know the situation), but it is crucial.

Implementation
It is customary to refer to the data requirements of ongoing activities as monitoring, used in a very narrow sense to refer to the quantitative review of physical and financial flows relative to planned targets. Such thinking focuses attention on inputs and outputs, rather than upon the

causal links between them or on equally significant linkages to the larger environment, which are all assumed to be self-evident. We prefer (as indicated in Table 4) to distinguish scanning from monitoring, and under the latter category to shift attention from mere gate measurement to what Stonecash terms 'withinputs' (cited in Saasa, 1985).

Box 2: Identifying all the stakeholders

It was to be a major project, the largest its donor operated in the country. Consequently all planning documents were signed by Treasury, the concerned technical Ministry, and the President's Office. This was important because incoming technical assistance staff were supposed to depend upon the Ministry for housing and transport, and the Administration for operating budgets and political direction.

Once the 'experts' arrived, however, they discovered how many interested agencies and parties had been overlooked. First, private rental housing had been nationalized and was formally under the Ministry of Lands and Housing, not the technical ministries. (There were already many other projects waiting for access to the housing they, too, had been promised.) Second, the Ministry of Works had no spare parts for the experts' vehicles, but no intention of letting them operate independently. Third, funds would have to receive approval of District and Provincial officials, who were not bound by national-level commitments. Fourth, the project structure did not accord with any yet established in the project area. It ignored the all-pervasive political party, but included low-status producers who held no legitimacy in the Government's own system.

In short, what had seemed to be a complete plan as negotiated in the capital city was badly flawed because so many key actors, at other levels, were either left out or else inappropriately placed within it.

Let us begin with a brief reference to *scanning*, the effort field managers put into watching general conditions in the environment where they work. Any experienced leader accustomed to working in turbulent conditions will know the many external factors relevant to good project performance: a project's standing within headquarters; whether this season's funds will arrive on time; the progress of the rainy season and hence condition of back-country roads; which project activities may be politically sensitive; and so forth. Changes which may threaten the attainment of current targets can arise form every direction. Effective managers become accustomed to keeping the larger environment under continuous surveillance (a function organization theorists term 'boundary scanning'). This necessity exists above and beyond the tracking of internal activities (or monitoring).

Once again we have a vital information-related function whose precise form and content cannot be predicted in advance. It is simply not feasible nor cost-effective to set up formalized surveillance covering all potential sources of stress. Instead, managers must rely upon qualitative understandings – largely developed from their own past experiences – to signal which changes in a rapidly changing overall situation merit an organized response.

Note, too, that the data which trigger an alarm can be either quantitative or qualitative. A collapse of commodity prices or an abrupt rise in interest rates may be just as threatening to a development project as, say, an unexpected change of minister. What matters is that external and internal conditions compete for managerial attention. When the burden of formal monitoring of internal activities becomes too great, field managers may fail to maintain adequate external surveillance. Thus the need for some degree of qualitative scanning always accompanies the ongoing implementation of rural development activities, whether recognized or not.

With regard to formal monitoring activities, Clayton (1983) has criticized the prevailing World Bank and UN monitoring concepts, pointing out that they focus on external gate measurements, rather than the process of project or agency implementation (see also Casley and Kumar, 1987). Gate measurements have two distinct limitations. First, while they may reveal a problem they are of little help in diagnosing the fault. Second, gate measurements may only reveal the presence of a problem when it is already too late to rectify.

These two problems are familiar enough even in a highly controlled factory environment where managers generally rely more on process rather than batch monitoring for quality control. Delays in correcting an assembly line fault can become very expensive, and only by watching processes as they occur can they learn how things start to go amiss. Gate measurements alone are insufficiently sensitive and timely. Given that the causal links between inputs and outputs in rural development are generally far more tenuous than in a factory, as well as subject to less control, the importance of process monitoring is at least as great. The next section considers some of the key internal and external agency-level variables that need to be monitored.

Detailed studies in high income countries of what managers actually do and how they obtain information, such as Mintzberg (1973), show that most spend a lot of time collecting informal information to guide their actions – contrary to their own *post hoc* rationalizations, which typically conform to theoretical notions of managerial functions (planning, budgeting, and so on). Face-to-face contacts with strategically placed observers both inside and outside their organizations are particularly important.

There is little reason to believe that practitioners of rural development in low and middle income countries are much different. Indeed, the typical gap between theory and practice is probably greater, though unfortunately there are few detailed studies which document how they do actually spend their time (Wiggins, 1992). However, our own experience is that informal enquiry is almost always the most important form of monitoring. For example, many senior managers or administrators will know which office staff have previously served in outlying areas and can be called upon quickly to give 'expert' views relating to that area. Too many decisions have to be taken in too little time to make it feasible to replace such informal enquiry with detailed quantitative surveys or monitoring systems – even arranging a meeting of field staff may take too long and be too expensive, particularly in sparsely populated areas where the geographical area involved is large.

Qualitative enquiry has a potential role not only in monitoring internal and external processes; it also may be useful for cross-checking the effectiveness of quantitative monitoring of inputs and outputs. Junior staff are very quick to respond, when their performance (and hence job security and pay) is being monitored relative to a particular quantitative target – that indeed is the strength of this approach. But they are also likely to be quick to find short cut ways of meeting such targets. The risks are particularly high when input estimates (area planted, farmers contacted, new loans disbursed etc) are used as proxy variables for target outputs (crop harvested, successful technology transfer, increased investment etc.).

A distinction that often appears in monitoring practice is between information required for ongoing management, and that required by funding organizations. Much formal monitoring is actually imposed upon local agencies by the latter, motivated by concerns about the need to be seen to be accountable for how money is being spent.

Thus, while externally-imposed monitoring systems may be highly comprehensive and elaborate, they also have inherent weaknesses. Information may be required to conform to particular summary tables and graphs used in headquarters for charting the achievements of field units. The summary tables contained in official reports often cannot be disaggregated to show local relationships, and thus are of no use to field managers supplying the data. Furthermore, comparisons of resources used and output achieved between field units become a justification for the supervisory unit itself. They are necessary, but do little to augment managerial capabilities while diverting senior staff time from the actual monitoring of field activities. They also have the powerful psychological

Box 3: Monitoring cattle dips for the Maasai

Let me illustrate the key difference between formal and informal monitoring. In the Maasai Project, we had to conform to standard district planning guidelines whenever projects were proposed which came out of the district budget (which most did). It was dictated to us from the District Development Director's office that, for financial reasons, six new dips (acaricide baths through which cattle are driven weekly to remove ticks) could be constructed each year. A lengthy process of planning and review determined which sites would have dips and what amounts the district would give for their construction. On one occasion we were told to build six dips in the same month that the District Development Director had removed all the transport for the building teams; and on another to build a dip where there were no ticks, against technical advice. A great deal of time was taken making the formal project planning procedures work, with little apparent benefit other then relieving the anxieties of higher level officials and party functionaries. That is, I suggest, the actual function of most formal monitoring.

At the same time, however, we were receiving numerous complaints from Maasai cattle owners about the operation of existing dips – of which we had 60, supplied and managed by the Livestock Development Department. Field visits told the same story: many dips not working, pumps broken, acaricide missing etc. This information when conveyed to district planners brought no response: only *new* projects were under the formal monitoring machinery. As project manager I finally went to the external donor to obtain extra funds, on a one-off basis, to bring in an external consultant to do a quick 'rough-and-ready' field survey. He did so within six weeks and reported in verbal debriefing that around 40 of the dips were not operational even though field staff continued to receive salaries as 'dip operators'. He gave a qualitative review of the causes of poor performance, mostly related to problems with water supplies and shoddy construction. But I never did receive a final report – a fact quite upsetting to the donor. To me, as manager, the verbal information was enough. It had confirmed our worst suspicions, and my own field visits supported the consultant's analysis of the reasons for dip failure. Having a questionnaire was necessary to give the review legitimacy; having a full analysis unnecessary except for justifying the use of funds and giving added leverage when talking to the district planners.

effect of reducing local managers' personal sense of responsibility and interest in the data they are required to furnish.

However, the principal danger of externally-imposed monitoring systems is that the staff and resource costs of running them are often underestimated by those who commission them. Modern organizations have a huge appetite for financial, time and activity reporting. This is made possible by computer technology, but motivated by the fact that failure to collect information is more likely to be punished than collection of too much – witness the time-sheets consultants routinely compile for the World Bank.

Evaluation

Some writers (e.g. Patton, 1980; 1990) use the word evaluation in a very broad sense to embrace all forms of action-oriented investigation. However, evaluation can generally be distinguished from broader research by its focus on the effect or impact of a specific intervention (though the conclusions of a good evaluation should, of course, feed into subsequent diagnosis and appraisal work).

Evaluation in this narrower sense has been categorized in numerous ways, usually along a broad spectrum that starts with enquiry into whether specific quantifiable goals have been achieved, passes through broader examination of the impact and effectiveness of a particular intervention (without restricting terms of reference to specific goals), and ends up with naturalistic enquiry – which is concerned with understanding detailed processes and borders on the domain of pure research. The appropriate mix of methods of enquiry, with increasing emphasis on qualitative methods, shifts as we move along the spectrum (Santo Pietro, 1983).

However, qualitative enquiry also has an important contribution to make to narrowly focused goal-based evaluations. This is most apparent when key project goals are themselves difficult to quantify, as is the case for example with social development projects that aim to address problems of access, exploitation, discrimination, low esteem, lack of participation, low awareness, and hopelessness among poor and marginalized people (Marsden and Oakley, 1990). Qualitative enquiry is also likely to be more appropriate for evaluation of projects with explicit *process* goals – in the field of public sector reform, for example – the full fruits of which are unlikely to fall within the project period, and are also difficult to forecast.

Even where goals are clearly defined and easily measured, it is often extremely difficult to establish the extent to which changes in them can be attributed unambiguously to the activity being evaluated using quantitative methods. To do so with any degree of statistical confidence, it is necessary to have data stretching back over time, and a large enough sample of observations (subject to differential levels of exposure to the activity under review) to permit reliable statistical analysis of the extent to which changes in target variables can be explained by what may be a very large set of endogenous and exogenous variables. Most statistical analysis, in short, ends up with qualitative interpretation of findings.

Nor does the potential importance of qualitative enquiry end there. Even if quantitative enquiry does yield strong conclusions about impact, a good evaluation also needs to address a whole series of detailed questions relating to particular strengths and weaknesses in project design and management. For example:

○ How did the quality of personnel affect key decisions and therefore eventual outcomes?
○ What were the subjective *perceptions* of different actors, and how did this affect eventual outcomes?
○ Why were there large gaps between targets and achieved performance?
○ What constitutes a *reasonable* level of performance under particular combinations of constraints?
○ How did politically-sensitive constraints (corruption, nepotism in staff selection etc.) affect performance?

The list could be extended greatly, and leads again to the conclusion that qualitative enquiry is not only useful, but indispensable at the evaluation stage. It frequently serves to counterbalance or explain adverse findings, so that any blame apportioned takes full account of extenuating local circumstances. However, it may also indicate where programme success is due to special factors which are unlikely to be present elsewhere.

Potentially one of the most useful lines of evaluation is comparative study of two or more interventions, with different characteristics maybe, but broadly similar goals. Many evaluators of rural development interventions find performance to be 'disappointing' but qualify their criticism by highlighting the harsh environment in which the intervention was located. The key evaluation question is then how well other, similar, programmes have fared under similar constraints. (Having access to this comparative perspective is especially important if the evaluators are themselves new to a given area.) It is usually fairly easy to arrange parallel visits and interviews, on an unofficial and 'off-the-record' basis, to give a valuable comparative perspective. One might visit staff housing provided in the area by other agencies, or talk to key informants about their perceptions of different programmes. Such sources can be very useful in judging the quality of effort and management in the programme or project being evaluated. Indeed, this comparative yardstick is often more useful than target attainment when assessing what documented levels of performance mean.

2.4 Some neglected variables

The foregoing discussion, particularly of monitoring, should have made it clear that to operate effectively practitioners need to collect a considerable amount of information, not only about farmers, villagers and the environment but also about their own and other institutions operating in the communities being served. The next two sections briefly review some of the variables that are often neglected in systematic rural enquiry, firstly at the agency level and secondly at the community level.

At the agency level

It is common, particularly in Sub-Saharan Africa, for outsiders to blame poor agency performance upon weak management, but such an 'explanation' may be merely a proxy for a host of constraints and difficulties. Some of these are listed in Table 5. The list is divided into two. The first set of variables relate to questions about other agencies operating in the same territory, such as:

o Do we co-operate with them or duplicate their services?
o Can our clients expect the support other agencies promise?
o Will their involvement with us negatively affect our activities?
o Do they have resources we might be able to tap, either by right, by special arrangement or in an emergency?
o Does this community really need our services, given the array already offered by other agencies?

To answer such questions, practitioners may need to enquire discretely and to visit the other agencies operating in the same area. The main points to be answered include:

o *Coverage*: how many agencies are already active and what is the approximate quality of their staff in each community?

o *Reliability*: which other agencies have the reputation or seem to have the resources to operate effectively? Can they be relied upon? Are their staff said to be corrupt? How corrupt?

o *Staff morale*: are field staff in a given agency likely to stay in post and provide services as expected? If morale is bad, why is it low and what implications does this hold for performance?

o *Past relations with farmers*: does the agency have good working relationships with farmers at the local level? Does it maintain contact groups which may have wider relevance?

○ *Specialities*: does the agency offer special services, either to particular client groups or to other agencies? Would use of such specialities be cheaper and more effective than providing them ourselves?

Such information can crucially affect programme planning at many points. Outside analysts often fail to recognize that most field programmes are interconnected, requiring for their success contributions from other units all through the crop growing and handling cycle. Range development programmes, for example, depend heavily upon adjunct water development, vehicle maintenance and livestock marketing services (which may be located in entirely different agencies). They also require general security and some degree of control over land use.

Whether we examine credit programmes, social forestry, fisheries development, or new crop introductions, the situation is the same: a matrix structure of interdependent service units. We find the paradox that while agencies are managed by strongly hierarchical devices, they actually operate in loosely coupled systems where one agency cannot order other units to comply with its plans.

Indeed, within a 'loosely coupled system' it may be counter-productive to employ managerial information technologies which assume a high degree of control over resources. Planning for other people not under one's control is a fundamentally different task from planning for one's own resources. Unfortunately, planning methodologies often assume the latter situation. Here Smith, Lethem and Thoolen (1980) offer some extraordinarily pertinent observations, based on a contrast they found between World Bank construction projects and rural development projects. In construction projects, conventional management techniques work well. Most of the critical resources are under project control and thus the information required is mainly of a progress monitoring type (network planning, completion indicators etc.). In rural development, on the contrary, project units control only a small sphere within the arena of potentially relevant factors. They must devote much more effort to keeping track of their environment and to those data which allow them to bargain with or otherwise influence the actions of other units. Thus the type of information needed changes between settings where a high degree of control exists and those where an agency is only one out of many which must cooperate to achieve their objectives. That is why answering the above questions about other units can be so important when formulating what strategy the agency should adopt.

The second cluster of agency variables listed in Table 5 relate to questions concerning the operations of a particular agency, its internal workings and ongoing performance. We can think of them as 'task' variables.

Table 5:   A checklist of neglected variables at the agency level

Organizational variation

Degree of financial support
Steep vs broad hierarchy
Spatial concentration of sites
Staff cleavages, polarization
Location of resources by level
Political leverage in system
Age and skills of labour force
Rigidity and formalism of in-house rules
Reporting, work, budgetary cycles
Objectives (single/multiple, clear/vague, realistic/unrealistic)
Relative size of top, middle, and bottom layers
Size and functions of 'technostructure' (staff)
Degree of professionalization of contact staff
Authority centralized or shared
Procedures and loads for dealing with clients

Task variation

Activities funded, by whom?
Technology vs labour intensive
Specificity of linked technological requirements
Degree governed by seasonality
Requires transport?
Skill levels required of staff? of clients?
Does output have high payoff?
Is effective performance visible?
What level of riskiness for client?
How sensitive to support risks?
What inputs required?
Single vs multiple functions
Degree of discretion required of staff? of clients?
Associated groups or leadership linkages?
Aim of handing tasks over to clients

Source: Adapted from Moris (1984)

Here there are many questions which managers may need to keep in mind, such as:

o Are the tasks being done of a nature that performance becomes plainly evident, either to farmers or to field staff?
o Are staff sufficiently motivated to work beyond regular hours or in difficult circumstances? Do tasks require such effort?
o Are there particular positions or cadres whose incumbents feel unfairly treated?
o Do staff feel their efforts are seen and appreciated by management?
o How are staff selected for transfer or for training?
o Is the organization building its future leadership and will it be able to hold such staff?
o Are financial expenditures staying with planned margins?
o Is the programme reaching all segments of the local community?
o Are particular requests from users/clients acted upon promptly and effectively?
o Is transport sufficient to get the job done?
o Are services or innovations being promoted in high local demand?

A manager taking up his or her position in a typical development agency soon learns that the organization's formal information-gathering processes are not designed to answer many of these questions. We face here the same input/output bias mentioned earlier: to a large extent, an agency's reporting data are prepared for the benefit of supervisors, not managers. In organizations which are not performance-oriented, the main function of such documentation seems at times to be to assuage supervisors' anxieties – one reason the documents may contain as much fiction as fact. Supervisors may not intend to act, but they do need to be reassured that field units are achieving something.

Official documentation thus has purposes quite unrelated to internal decisionmaking and so to management's actual needs for information. It is meant to prove that no funds have been expended without proper authority; to document nights out spent by senior staff in the field; to list staff transfers, movements and retirements and the like: purposes with still apparent roots in colonial systems. Such details are time consuming to compile, especially when modernized to incorporate ill-chosen, quantitative performance accounting. Usually the annual report and financial statements must be signed by senior management; they are meant to render such staff accountable to the organization's headquarters.

Perhaps such intentions are necessary and laudable. They do not, however, assist field managers in making their own strategic decisions unless considerable thought has been devoted to the precise format and timing of such reports in relation to actual decisionmaking needs. This point cannot be stressed too strongly. For example, in many public agencies the accounting system (which is imposed by statute) is mainly directed towards proving wrong-doing. Such an intention has no linkage to current management at all and, in actual fact, the audited accounts may not be returned to field managers until years afterward.

There are obvious reforms which some agencies have introduced: confidential staff performance reports which are prepared jointly with the person concerned; annual works plans for all senior staff; cost centres chosen for their functional significance and reported in a way which shows current cash flows and balances at a glance; introduction of realistic transfer cost pricing, to track where money is actually being spent within internal operations; and so forth.

Otherwise, managers are left mainly to rely upon qualitative and informal information sources to guide their actions (the monitoring of current cash balances at the bank perhaps the one outstanding exception). A wise field manager will devote at least some attention to the following features (with feedback from diverse sources):

O staff morale and turnover;
O availability and condition of transport;
O rate of expenditure, by category, project and location;
O quality of incoming staff;
O ability to meet scheduling targets;
O progress being achieved on construction projects;
O any reports of corruption;
O service popularity in given communities;
O evidence of staff initiative;
O evidence of time spent in the field.

These are all things which to some degree come under managerial control. They are thus considerably more use as indicators of performance than the usual output targets which purport to show demonstrated impact (e.g. tonnes harvested, etc.). They are obviously not 'variables' in the research sense, but they are significant indicators of organizational well-being.

In summary, the failure to look at agency features can have serious negative consequences for rural development. First, any intervention which depends for its success on other agencies can be jeopardized if their likely performance has been wrongly assessed. Second, with strongly hierarchical field agencies where staff may have vastly different qualifications, motivations and resources, there is often a large gap between what those at the top intend and what actually occurs at the bottom. Having access to good information about an agency's internal workings is vital to the design of any reform measures. And third, where there are so many environmental problems, managers have little incentive to learn from their mistakes. To say what can be achieved means viewing organizational activities in a comparative context against the backdrop of actual performance being achieved by other agencies under similar constraints.

At the community level

Those who work with rural communities on a continuing basis find that certain issues arise again and again within field programmes. There is, for example, the 'big man' syndrome: the necessity when dealing with villagers of securing the backing of influential locals. Sometimes factionalism – an internal polarization of the community into rival social groups – must be allowed for and even counteracted. On other occasions, service staff encounter 'adopted' or 'pet' villages – communities which receive help not because of their needs but because they are known and liked by district officials, or perhaps a Minister in the national government. In many rural areas, people have become accustomed to waiting passively for external interventions as an answer to all problems. This 'dependency syndrome' makes them unwilling to act together on even minor problems which could be solved by their own actions. In other places field staff must counteract the attitudinal 'backwash' created by urbanization, which can cause people to undervalue local opportunities and to demand 'modern', technologically sophisticated interventions even where these are unnecessary.

Such factors are pervasive and powerful; they have real consequences. Nevertheless, they are not easily demonstrated by means of the usual field survey. Indeed, rural decisionmakers typically find little which is of direct, operational use in the results of the typical multi-subject farm/household survey. Partly, this gap can be explained because of the measurement difficulties associated with factors of this kind. Those who design survey instruments for monitoring and evaluation have tended to focus on obvious variables like farm size, crop yields and household traits; they are unaccustomed to measuring complex political and attitudinal factors. However, the gap also occurs because the factors themselves do not vary at the farm and household levels: they refer to properties of the community rather than of individual farms. If in field studies no separate attempt has been made to document community traits, inevitably such factors will remain 'invisible' and thus not be systematically considered.

What are the key community traits which rural planners and service managers may need to know about? Obvious candidates from the authors' own experience would include the following.

o *Aggregate cash flow*: whether there is sufficient cash turnover in a community to support various economic activities of a secondary and tertiary nature. Often, in subsistence agriculture, there isn't. In a more commercialized setting, high levels of aggregate indebtedness among farm families may also sharply constrain cash flows.

o *Main sources of cash income*: whether cash is derived from local opportunities or from long distance labour migration matters a great deal. In a 'remittance economy' households may lack both the funds and the authority to invest and there will be little cash turnover to tax. Which crops people depend upon determines their calendar of activities, when shortages of labour and food will occur and how they are paid: critical facts to the service organization.

o *Previous development efforts*: the record of projects and activities already attempted in an area can strongly influence how people react to new proposals. It is also a useful indicator for judging the chances of success of new initiatives.

o *Past money management*: whether local leaders have already paid back project loans, or otherwise demonstrated an ability to raise and manage their own funds.

o *Infrastructure*: breakdowns in a particular service agency do not matter as much if there are alternatives readily at hand. Communities vary greatly in their degree of service and infrastructure. What is needed is a rough idea of the aggregate level of institutional non-performance, a type of riskiness just as important to farmers as are natural production risks. For agricultural projects with a focus on new technology, the reliability of power and water supply are particularly important.

o *Community leadership traits*: whether stable community leadership actually exists. Whether they can be trusted, and are they trusted locally? Are there rivals waiting in the wings? Have they fulfilled on previous promises, or will they require prodding at each stage? Who are the local 'Big Men'?

o *Degree of inequality and factionalism*: where land and income are unevenly distributed, or factionalism prevalent, farmers may be reluctant to participate in joint projects. Then even routine administrative choices, such as appointment of staff or the location of a facility, can become politically charged. Statements (especially common in Africa) that the social culture is 'egalitarian' should not be taken literally (Grandin, 1988).

o *Degree of corruption*: when either local leaders or service staff are seen to be corrupt, this perception complicates many aspects of programme operation. What to do about operational delays, whether to participate in local pay-offs and similar considerations require astute judgement about systematic functioning.

○ *Security situation*: this affects staff movements and postings, how money is handled and the degree of effort devoted to safeguarding equipment and facilities. It obviously also affects farmers' decisions, affecting the marketing of commodities but also whether they are willing to hold vulnerable assets (like dairy cows).

The above factors are not, strictly speaking 'variables': they refer to clusters of concern, each of which may have several interrelated components. A more extended listing was given earlier, in Table 2. We should expect that the concerns which merit priority attention will vary according to the type of programme, the community in which it is located and certain regional features typical of different parts of the world.

There are several reasons for calling community variables invisible. Usually these factors are omitted from farm-level field surveys, either through a failure to consider supra-farm variation or because the variables are themselves difficult to document. Consequently, unless an extra effort is made, they will remain in the background, unexamined and unaddressed. They then emerge after project and programme decisions have been made, becoming potent obstacles which may continue to confound subsequent implementation efforts. Additionally, some of these variables are quite literally invisible: they cannot be seen by direct inspection. Even when project and programme designers visit a community, they will fail to recognize some of its most pertinent features.

This perhaps explains why technicians often view political factors as being primarily a negative influence, to be circumvented during planning and opposed during implementation. For example, in many fields of rural development planning, site locations will be determined to suit technical criteria: quality of soils, density of population, disease risks, water availability and so forth. With so many stringencies to satisfy, project planners are loath to consider political criteria as well. And yet the locations of facilities determines major political impacts, influencing who can claim credit (at the district and national levels), where staff will live (and thus various income transfer effects) and who will be the immediate beneficiaries (through sale of land, construction contracts and casual employment). There is nothing intrinsically negative or mysterious about such considerations. They are rational and *they can be predicted*. Local leaders usually have stable political interests and a knowable constituency (why in public policy they are termed 'stakeholders'). Political variables thus become obstacles when they are left unexamined and unarticulated until after key location decisions have been reached. Then, indeed, project implementation may discover the local politicians oppose their every move and even take strenuous steps to relocate or abort the project.

The point is surely that technical staff usually do not have direct access to the kinds of information which are relevant at the community level. If they fail to examine such phenomena, the price will be that field activities generate unnecessary opposition, that projects and programmes are badly located, that activities and services may be inappropriate to local needs and field staff may be left to fight against ingrained pressures and negative tendencies which could have been avoided. The main advantage of 'participatory planning' whether it adopts quantitative or qualitative methods, is that it opens the door for considering these otherwise invisible factors at an early stage in the policy/project cycle.

It is easier to see that the necessary village-level information is primarily qualitative if we anticipate the questions which must be answered when operating within a village. Let us take as an example the installation of a rural water supply (here see Cairncross *et al.* 1980). Questions which would immediately arise might include:

O What permission(s) must be obtained to work on the site?
O Who would own the completed facility?
O What technical surveys will be needed?
O Can local contractors do the jobs required in construction?
O What contributions can the people make and how should these be organized?
O Where will finds be held and how will they be distributed?
O Where can supplies be held if the people do the work?
O Who will do the site mapping and layout?
O How will those who lose land be compensated?
O Who will operate and maintain the completed facility?

Again, this is only a partial list from among many potential questions. We can readily appreciate the implementors' desire to achieve closure by concentrating on a few key issues. Indeed, the usual pattern is for a central Ministry or Water Supply Board to shoulder all technical responsibilities, perhaps even insisting upon a standard design and allowing almost no local input into the design and construction process. The consequence is equally predictable: while the central agency can build many supplies in each funding period, a good number will be wrongly or poorly sited, the people will have little commitment to the projects sited in their area, and there will be no local maintenance which is not paid for externally. Within a few years, many of the supplies built in this fashion will be inoperable and derelict, awaiting a new round of donor-financed centralized support (see an excellent study of rural water supplies in Tanzania by Therkildsen, 1988).

A more participatory approach to communal involvement in rural service provision will be less efficient in the short-run, but possibly more effective in the long run. The goal changes from being simply the provision of service x (a domestic water point, a cattle dip, a bridge and so forth) to enhancing local capabilities through the process of creating an added facility. This goal, in turn, requires greater interaction between service providers and clients and thus a two-way flow of information about many aspects which could be ignored in a standard 'top-down' approach.

The need to acquire comprehensive information on these invisible aspects can be just as pressing after the fact of intervention, when perhaps a service agency must determine why earlier initiatives have not been effective. In a poor, developing country, there will be an enormous number of possible reasons to explain low project and programme performance. Obviously, any remedies adopted will be ineffective if they address the wrong causes, or if they deal with only a few out of several interconnected constraints. And yet agency staff cannot afford to examine all possible causes with cumbersome and expensive field surveys. What they typically do instead (if they employ any systematic approach to data acquisition) is to seek out key informants in the local system. By this means they rapidly narrow the scope for potential change to a few critical dimensions, thereby using in fact if not in name a form of 'rapid rural appraisal'. Thus organizational remedies need field screening just as much as farm-level technologies do; the process of qualitative enquiry to identify the key local constraints is quite similar in either context.

2.5 Criteria for effective information supply

We can conclude this review of practitioners' needs for rural information with a list of key criteria for the evaluation of rural enquiry methodologies, which is adapted from a list of criteria for approaches to monitoring suggested by Wilson (1983, cited in Coleman, 1987b:107). Rural enquiry should aim:

○ to be holistic and comprehensive;
○ to deliver information direct to the appropriate level of management;
○ to be cost effective;
○ to pay particular regard to the opportunity cost of staff time;
○ to relate to targets and goals;
○ to be operationally relevant;
○ to be timely;
○ to be reliable.

That considerable scope exists for improving rural enquiry in terms of these criteria is illustrated by the enormous variation in current practice between (and even within) different organizations. It is said, to give a particularly extreme example, that the Chinese Government could have built Somalia's Bardeere Dam for the same amount that the World Bank spent simply carrying out preliminary surveys!

34

Another factor behind current variation in information handling practice is the differential spread in the application of modern information technology and business practice. A tremendous expansion in computerized data handling, and formalization of management information systems (with its own academic and professional devotees) is characteristic of modern organizations. The practice of rural development has not been left out; the rapid spread (initially through donor agencies) of formal appraisal, monitoring and evaluation methodology based on the project cycle being perhaps the leading example (see Section 4.2). As these procedures become more complicated and (it is claimed) rigorous, they generate new types of information as a product, but also have high upstream and downstream costs, particularly in their demands on the time of skilled staff. Such innovations therefore needs to be carefully appraised, against lower-cost alternatives, including greater reliance on qualitative methods – the nature of which it is now necessary to describe.

3 The Nature of Qualitative Enquiry

3.1 A rapid literature review

Qualitative enquiry has been used and written about by people from an exceptionally wide range of backgrounds and perspectives. Patton (1990), for example, distinguishes between ten 'theoretical traditions' with roots in disciplines ranging from anthropology and psychology, to theology and theoretical physics! While some of these traditions may be of little direct relevance to practitioners of rural development, his list also excludes geographers, educationists, historians, economists, organization theorists, political scientists and no doubt writers from other disciplines who have made useful contributions to the literature. The rapid review that follows is therefore highly selective, and perhaps also somewhat biased by the fact that the bulk of our own working experience has been related to agriculture.

Social science research
The most formidable body of literature on qualitative enquiry is concerned with its application to social science research, particularly as carried out by sociologists, social psychologists and anthropologists. While much of this material is based on fieldwork in rural areas of low income countries, it has been directed principally at an academic audience, and concerned more with establishing truth than with influencing specific management or policy decisions. Standard texts include van Maanen (1983), Patton (1990), Wengle (1988), Whyte (1989), Fielding and Fielding (1986), Haberman (1978), Cook and Reichardt (1979) and Johnson (1975). Critical examinations of the epistemology of applied research include Glaser and Strauss (1967), Scott and Shore (1979), Argyris *et al.* (1987), and Leiter (1980).

Most of these books discuss both theoretical issues and the strengths and weaknesses of different qualitative methods; including participant observation, case-studies, identification of key informants, in-depth interviewing, focused group discussions, study of documents and artifacts and so on. Other texts focus mostly on methods, or on one particular technique; including Kearl (1976), Hursh-Cesar and Roy (1976) and Brewer and Hunter (1989). The publishers Sage have produced more than twenty small handbooks in a specific series on Qualitative Research Methods, including McCracken (1988) on the extended interview, Morgan (1988) on focus groups, and Wolcott (1990) on writing up. Casley and Kumar (1988) and Kumar (1987) both present an outline of qualitative methods within the social sciences, written explicitly for practitioners. Lastly, Devereux and Hoddinott (1993) give an especially useful introduction.

It is interesting to note the widespread reference to data acquisition within this tradition as fieldwork. Most closely associated with anthropologists, the term implies that good data depend upon the insights, skills and interpretive acumen of the investigator – a job which is therefore hard to delegate. The term also enables authors to escape committing themselves to a single quantitative or qualitative methodology.

Table 6 provides a short checklist to illustrate how fieldwork strategies may vary.

Table 6:   Fieldwork strategies

Role of the enquirer
Participation – Observation

Portrayal of the enquirer's role to others
Overt – Covert

Focus of the enquiry
Open – Predetermined (e.g. fully coded questionnaire)

Portrayal of the focus of the enquiry
Open – Covert/false

Duration of the enquiry
Short-term/single visit – Long-term/multiple visits

Source: adapted from Patton (1987)

Many qualitative researchers have in the past made a virtue of not entering the field with a specific policy agenda in mind, fearing that this would colour their perceptions. This, and primary orientation to their academic peer group, has hindered the timely flow of relevant findings to practitioners (here see criticisms of 'academics' by Chambers, 1983b).

More recently, however, the barrier between academic research and practice has begun to diminish, partially through a reassessment by academic anthropologists and sociologists themselves of the need for closer engagement (e.g. Booth, 1992); and also through increased employment of sociologists and anthropologists within aid organizations (see, for example, Cernea, 1990; Sutherland, 1987).

Closer engagement is also being facilitated by increased adoption of qualitative research methodology by specialists in applied fields. Education policy, for example, traditionally relied upon quantitative source of data for monitoring and evaluation, and focused on policy and planning, while neglecting actual implementation. Research by educationalists using qualitative methods, however, has begun to restore balance by providing policy makers with more feedback from the 'chalk face.' (Finch, 1986; Burgess, 1985; Vulliamy et al., 1990).

Rapid rural appraisal

Rapid rural appraisal (RRA), encompasses a much wider range of tasks than interpretation of the term 'appraisal' in its narrow economic sense (ex ante analysis prior to investment) suggests, and this has prompted suggestions for alternative names. For example, Honadle (1982) refers to 'rapid rural reconnaissance' and Cernea (1990) to 'rapid assessment procedures' (RAP). However, the RRA label, originating from conferences at the Institute of Development Studies in Brighton in 1978 and 1979, seems to have stuck. Key papers were published in a special IDS Bulletin, edited by Chambers in 1981.

RRA grew in large measure out of farming systems research (FSR); more specifically out of the problem of how to classify farmers into homogeneous groups, and identify key production constraints within each (Collinson, 1972; Rhoades, 1982; Hildebrand, 1981; Zandstra, 1979). Confronted with a huge array of potentially relevant variables and a largely illiterate client group, researchers were forced to make hard choices about how the limited time and resources available for information acquisition could be used most efficiently. Rigorous surveys were not only costly and time consuming – 'survey slavery' as Chambers (1983:51) called it – they also assumed that researchers already knew the key questions (out of the thousands they could ask) that should be included in their questionnaires. Ad hoc and informal or 'quick-and-dirty' methods of data collection, on the other hand, often amounted to little more than rural development tourism, to quote Chambers again ((1983).

Early RRA, that developed in the context of farming systems research, included:

O intensive fieldwork in a particular area over a few weeks carried out by a multidisciplinary team;

38

o informal farmer surveys carried out by one or two senior investigators over several weeks, in place of more comprehensive but time-consuming quantitative surveys carried out by specially recruited field investigators (Collinson, 1972).

However, the precise fieldwork method was less important than recognition of the need to arrive at a rough approximation of the value of many variables within a complex system in order to be able to decide what to focus on in more detail through more specialized studies. The optimum strategy might involve successive approximations, attained by applying a mixture of methods and disciplines, in order to eliminate rival hypotheses and to focus upon key aspects where further investigatory work is most needed. As such, RRA emerged not as a *method* at all, but as a *strategy* for exploratory work where there are unknowns.

It quickly became apparent that this form of intermediate technology was appropriate not only to agricultural research, but to most aspects of rural development. The general principal is neatly captured by the concept of an optimal level of ignorance (Ilchman, 1972). Ilchman contends that in rural policymaking we usually deal with many unknowns. While the returns to a little effort spent on acquiring new information are high, the cost per unit of information acquired goes up dramatically as we begin to insist on higher standards of data comprehensiveness and quality. In the language of micro-economics, the marginal returns to more open enquiry, are often greater than the marginal returns to more focused enquiry. Practitioners face the dilemma of deciding when enough is known to proceed – or what level of ignorance can be afforded?

Once this point was accepted the RRA literature expanded rapidly, absorbing relevant ideas from anthropology and numerous other sources, including agroecosystem analysis carried out by Conway and others in Southeast Asia, and participatory approaches to rural enquiry conducted by BRAC (1980) in Bangladesh. A second major conference was held in 1985 at Khon Kaen University, Thailand (with papers published by USAID in 1987). By then it had acquired a distinct toolkit of techniques, and a clear philosophy, summed up by the '5i's' (McCracken, Pretty, Conway, 1988:13):

1. iterative – goals and processes modified through learning by doing;
2. innovative – techniques adapted to each new problem, rather than applied according to a fixed procedure;
3. interactive – interdisciplinary;
4. informal – avoiding use of predetermined questionnaires;
5. in the community – learning taking place through exchange of ideas with rural people in the field.

Since the mid-eighties, much of the innovation within RRA (with several Indian NGOs in the vanguard) has focused in particular on finding ways of strengthening participation not only in the process of investigation, but where possible also in follow-up action (IIED/MYRADA, 1991). Thus RRA is increasingly referred to as Participatory Rural Appraisal, or PRA. When applied to the original field of agricultural research, PRA has combined with research findings on the importance of indigenous technical knowledge (ITK) to develop the concept of 'farmer-participatory research', which seeks to draw upon farmers' own experience and expertise by involving them not only in data collection and diagnosis, but also in carrying out and evaluating experiments – an approach discussed in Section 4.1.

Meanwhile, the general RRA/PRA toolkit expanded to include wealth ranking; construction of village or watershed transects, maps, models, seasonal calendars and other diagrams; use of aerial photographs; pairwise or matrix ranking of technology options; and more familiar qualitative methods borrowed from the social sciences such as semi-structured interviewing of key informants, participant observation, and discussion with focus groups. A number of detailed case-books have also been produced, including: IIED/MYRADA (1991), McCracken, Pretty, Conway (1988), and back-copies of *RRA Notes* produced by the International Institute for Environment and Development (IIED).

However, experience in using some of these techniques is still relatively limited (particularly within government agencies), and potential problems, include:

○ disillusionment among villagers if early enthusiasm and expectations (stimulated by PRA in particular) are not followed up;
○ disillusionment among practitioners when using some of the more demanding techniques without adequate training or induction, particularly when making contact with particular communities for the first time;
○ their application to communities in conflict, suggesting the need for more interface between RRA/PRA and the disciplines of counselling, mediation and conflict-resolution.

Evaluation of social development projects
Social development, as defined for example by Oxfam (Pratt and Boyden, 1985), refers to sustainable improvements in individual and community self-reliance, or their capacity to sustain their own development. It includes:

○ becoming more aware of factors inhibiting development and self-reliance;

○ reducing dependence on (or exploitation by) landowners, traders, benevolent aid organizations and others;
○ overcoming negative attitudes towards self-help, including fear, lack of confidence, fatalism, suspicion and superstition;
○ increasing solidarity and cohesion with others in a similar situation, and strengthening institutions for collective action.

Fostering such changes has become an increasingly explicit development goal, particularly of NGOs, where Korten's three-fold classification of development strategies (e.g. 1987:148) has been particularly influential. This classifies NGOs according to whether their primary orientation is either: relief and welfare at the individual and household level (first generation); self-help income-raising projects at the community level (second generation), or advocacy and establishment of sustainable systems at regional or national level (third generation).

Relief and welfare goals can more easily be broken down into neat projects with clearly defined target groups, and tangible and measurable objectives, such as more food, better housing, and improved services. But achieving such goals affords little satisfaction if the success cannot be sustained once external support is withdrawn, while to guarantee that support indefinitely may undervalue local resources and capabilities. Refocusing on social development goals may therefore be seen as an effort to increase the effectiveness of external support over a longer period. However, the tangible effects cannot be accurately predicted; in part because uncertainty increases with the time horizon, and in part because 'target groups' themselves have more say in eventual outcomes. Measuring performance against final products is therefore almost impossible, and it becomes necessary to fall back on process goals – including social development as defined above. Thus while social development may be valued as an end in itself, it can also be justified in many contexts as a means to more tangible ends. Finsterbusch and van Wicklin (1989), for example, provide evidence that the degree of participation by intended beneficiaries was positively correlated with the performance of a sample of 52 USAID projects.

Many NGOs have been quicker to embrace social development than governments or official donors; and this may indeed be a factor behind the widespread belief in their greater cost-effectiveness. However, as they have grown in importance and come to rely more on government funding, they have come under increasing pressure to demonstrate that this is actually so; and this challenge that has acted as a catalyst to discussion of evaluation. Process goals, social development, and third-generation strategies are all inherently more difficult to measure and evaluate, yet there is growing recognition (within NGOs as well from sceptical observers) that more and better evaluation is a priority for them; see for example Sen (1987). The issue has already spawned a very considerable literature – see, for example, Marsden and Oakley (1990), which is based on a conference on 'the evaluation of social development projects' held in Swansea in 1989, the papers of which are also published in a special issue (Vol. 6, No. 4) of the *Community Development Journal.*

Two distinct strands can be distinguished in this literature. The first strand accepts the need for more reliable or externally verifiable evaluation to satisfy outsiders that funds allocated to process-oriented development activities are being well spent. Harding (1991:294) advocates monitoring of various quantifiable indicators of social development (for example, the number of local institutions in existence, number of meetings, attendance at meetings, measures of the scale of activities undertaken); an approach also favoured by Oxfam (Pratt and Boyden, 1985).

A danger of exclusive reliance on such targets, is that staff may concentrate on achieving them at the expense of quality (cf. Section 2.3). An alternative approach hinted at by Brown (1991) is to focus on awareness-building as a key element of social development by finding ways of monitoring changes in the sharing of information between rural development agencies and their client groups. Where lack of information is an important element of powerlessness this has inherent strength, but it leaves unanswered the problem of how the extent of information-sharing can accurately be monitored.

Others favour subjective ranking or scoring of qualitative changes against an agreed checklist of criteria. Damodaram (1991) for example suggests that each development activity or situation should be evaluated for increased awareness, confidence, leadership, independence, bargaining capacity and desire for better living. Finsterbusch and van Wicklin (1987), on the other hand, have produced a longer checklist for the evaluation of participation within the project cycle, reproduced in Table 7, and suggest ascribing each a score on a scale of one to seven.

Such approaches have obvious practical utility, but they should be seen as no more than examples of the point at which different evaluators have decided to put numbers on qualitative data, with the consequent trade-off between loss of information and ease of manipulation as discussed in Section 1.2. In other words, they are illustrative of a more general point, which is the need to incorporate aspects of qualitative methodology (as discussed in Section 3.1) into evaluation – a point which seems self-evident to some writers on qualitative methods who use the words evaluation and research almost interchangeably (e.g. Patton, 1987 and 1990); though not to others (e.g. Brewer and Hunter, 1989 for whom 'evaluation research is the 'new' tool linking policymakers and social scientists').

Table 7:   Indicators for the evaluation of participation

A. Beneficiaries' role in the planning phase

1. Degree of participation in original idea
2. Degree of participation in project planning
3. Beneficiary commitment to the project

B. Beneficiaries' role in implementation phase

4. Degree of financial contribution
5. Degree of participation in implementation
6. Degree of indigenous knowledge used vs dependency on outside experts
7. Degree of organisation of beneficiaries
8. Extent to which organisation is 'theirs' vs engineered by others

C. Beneficiaries' role in maintenance phase

9. Degree of participation in maintenance
10. Degree of indigenous knowledge used vs dependency on outside experts after project completion
11. Degree of local vs outside ownership and control of facilities and organisations

Source: Finsterbusch and van Wicklin (1987)

The problem of how outsiders can evaluate social development, however, is only one element of this literature. The starting point for the second and more important strand is the realization that the process of evaluation is itself an important social development tool. Participatory evaluation, or self-evaluation (Uphoff, 1991) may be a powerful catalyst of social development by helping to create awareness, collective responsibility and solidarity. Korten (1980) argues that because rural development programmes must operate in a dynamic, unstable environment those which succeed do so by learning how to 'embrace error' constructively. There is therefore an important distinction to be drawn between internal and external evaluation of social development (Howes, 1991).

A participatory self-evaluation procedure adopted by FAO for the People's Participation Programme, developed by Uphoff (1991), for example, starts with a process of consultation to arrive at a list of relevant questions that each farmers' group should consider. The groups are then asked to give themselves a score, ranging from four (little room for improvement) to zero (unacceptable, need for drastic improvement) at the other. These scores can then be used as an internal benchmark for each group to review its position in the following year, as well as for external and numerical comparisons.

Since the prime purpose of evaluation is to inform future decisions, the balance between internal and external evaluation is linked to the more fundamental issue of power and authority within different organizations discussed in Section 2.1. Howes (1991) and Hocksbergen (1986) also relate it to the wider challenge to the modernization paradigm, which views development largely as the transfer of superior technology, requiring external initiation and supervision.

Policy analysis
Just as in the 1970s donors incorporated project appraisal into the routine preparation of field programmes, so in the 1980s they began to add policy analysis and social impact assessment. Essentially, to do this requires driving estimates of policy outcomes from figures which represent social and economic costs and benefits, as well as impacts. There are methodologies coming into widespread use which show how this can be done for rural development in the Third World: notably Monke and Pearson (1989), Derman and Whiteford (1985), Conyers (1982), Finsterbusch et al. (1990), and White (1990).

Furthermore, the standard approaches used for analytic purposes in developed countries deal with many of the same issues as in less developed countries (LDCs). Thus practitioners of Third World rural development can find standard developed country sources like Patton and Sawicki (1986, Chapters 1 and 2), Finsterbusch and Motz (1980), Branch et al. (1984), and Leistritz and Murdock (1981) quite useful. These methodologies provide a means of synthesis to weigh one option against another; they do not, unfortunately, provide raw data. Here we find typically that some or all of the key facts are missing, and must be inserted by those on the spot as the analysis proceeds. Ideally, we might request policymakers to wait until the necessary policy research has been carried out. In practice, they will usually proceed with whatever information they have in hand supplemented by analysts' own 'best guesses' for missing variables and parameters (Patton and Sawicki, 1986).

If so (and we do believe this is what commonly occurs), why not turn to RRA and qualitative enquiry rather than the analysts' own hunches? The strengths of qualitative enquiry are precisely the ones needed in this instance, since qualitative methods are designed to draw upon multiple information sources of varying quality, and are meant to yield results quickly. When the preliminary review so indicates, it may be necessary to wait until high quality, quantitative data can be compiled. On the other hand, the range of values provided by a quick-and-dirty qualitative review may be sufficient for application of sensitivity analysis, and this in turn may suggest that further refinement of the data base will not be cost-effective. Field workers should anticipate that policy analysis, social impact assessment, and environmental impacts will be applied routinely within most forms of development planning in the near future. We consider qualitative enquiry to be highly suited to these purposes, replacing mere guesswork but sometimes becoming the prelude to more extended enquiry when the issues at stake merit such investment.

Parallel developments in quantitative enquiry.
In order to provide some balance, it is important to note that while the literature on qualitative enquiry for rural development has been expanding along the lines discussed above, the far larger literature on quantitative enquiry has not stood still. Developments in the application of quantitative methods to rural enquiry include:

O further elaboration of appraisal, monitoring and evaluation procedures within the project cycle, including wider adoption and adaptation of the *logical framework* (see Section 4.2).
O the introduction of increasingly large and complex programme surveys – to fill gaps in *social accounting matrices* for monitoring the social dimensions of adjustment in Sub-Saharan Africa, for example World Bank (1991);
O the evaluation of extension programmes through surveys of *knowledge, attitudes and practices* (KAP) stemming from the work of Everett Rogers and others on technology diffusion during the sixties (Rogers, 1983);
O the refinement of conventional *farm management surveys* with a view to improving identification of agricultural research priorities – including yield gap analysis (see Section 4.3), decision-tree approaches (Barlett, 1980), and models of farmer response in uncertainty (Stewart, 1986);

3.2   Some unifying principles

What common ground exists between the three major strands of literature on qualitative enquiry discussed above? A short answer, that also serves as a caveat to more ambitious generalization, is that qualitative enquiry in all its current manifestations emphasizes *diversity*, on at least two levels.

1. There is a general acceptance that the techniques of enquiry must be adapted to the decisions they are intended to inform and the context in which they are made.
2. There is also widespread recognition that the quality and reliability of

information can be enhanced by using more than one source of data or technique of enquiry – a methodological principal generally referred to as 'triangulation' (Denzin, 1970).

At the same time, this methodological pluralism is not advanced as a licence for *ad hoc* or haphazard methods. All writers also agree that careful preparation and professionalism are essential ingredients of good qualitative enquiry. This section discusses these three issues – pluralism, triangulation, and professionalism – in more detail. Section 3.4 then draws upon our own working experience to discuss practical difficulties arising from use of particular sources of information.

Methodological pluralism
Qualitative methods can be classified in various ways, and each text book differs slightly in its approach. At the most general level, for example, Patton (1990) argues that qualitative methods all rely on just three underlying forms of data collection: open-ended interviews, direct observation, and review of documents. Diversity arises from the specification of more detailed procedures that are appropriate to more particular tasks; the need for depth or breadth, openness or confidentiality, and so on (Patton, 1987).

Whyte (1977), on the other hand, classifies an array of field techniques according to whether they are oriented towards:

O observation;
O questioning and listening;
O intervention and measurement.

Observation emphasizes the situation, whereas questioning emphasizes the respondent. Intervention often yields the most conclusive results, but is the also the most intrusive. Cross-cutting all three approaches is the degree to which they depend upon accompanying content analysis, which can be either qualitative or quantitative. Whyte (1977) goes on to illustrate the range of possibilities by providing a cross-tabulation of 14 important system variables against which 24 data collection methods potentially apply. Half her variables can be described by seven or more field methods. She also provides rough estimates of the time requirement for each field method.

While differences may emerge over how methods of qualitative enquiry can best be categorized or over the most appropriate task for a specific job, serious debate about the general superiority of one method over another – participant observation versus interviewing, for example (Trow, 1957) – has long ceased to arouse passions. Moreover, methodological pluralism generally extends to include quantitative techniques of enquiry as well, despite continued debate over the practical implications of underlying epistemological differences (induction versus deduction etc.).

The text on qualitative methods in Third World educational research by Vulliamy, Lewin and Stephens (1990) provides an interesting example. The book first rejects '...the assumption that relatively unambiguous procedures can be laid down for novice researchers to follow, whatever the context in which the research takes place.' Instead each author presents a personal case study of a particular research project, and relates it to their own disciplinary backgrounds and methodological preferences. Lancy (1993), also reviewing educational applications, presents eight distinct perspectives but devotes most attention to four: case studies, personal accounts, cognitive studies, and historical enquiry.

Underlying such pluralism is a tacit acceptance that knowledge derived from one method of enquiry, or associated with one discipline, is always only a partial approximation to the whole truth; a view that is increasingly shared by philosophers of natural science, too (Patton, 1987). If many researchers are prepared to humble themselves this much, then practitioners of rural development should be equally pragmatic, given that they are generally even more constrained in their data collection by institutional context, time and resources.

Triangulation

Methodological pluralism raises the question of what happens when two separate lines of enquiry throw up contradictory evidence. In some cases, discrepancies can confidently be attributed to bias or weakness in one technique or the other, in which case using more than one technique increases the reliability of overall findings. Often, however, the discrepancies provide useful hints that lead to synthesis and to deeper insights. Dividing available resources between more than one method therefore often results in more reliable and insightful data.

The term sociologists apply to this strategy is triangulation (see Denzin, 1970). It can take several forms: using different methods to cross-check a result; different theories to explain outcomes; different investigators to test quality; and different subjects, varying in scope, time and space (Ianni and Orr, 1979, citing Denzin). An extended illustration is provided in Box 4.

As Denzin predicts, the field worker employing triangulations can encounter puzzling results which defy easy explanation. Trend (1978) reports a classic review of three US direct cash housing allowance experiments, one of which was carefully documented using both quantitative and qualitative approaches. The initial qualitative report, based on more than 25,000 pages of written notes submitted by resident observers, came to strikingly different conclusions from those based on

Box 4:   Triangulation in Upper Embu District, Kenya

My own PhD research (Moris, 1970) employed triangulation, though without calling it such: three seasons of mainly quantitative, practice adoption surveys in several central Kenyan communities; some parallel interviewing, both of farmers and key informants; extended residence in two areas, allowing some participant observation; and a subsequent, exhaustive review of the daily records for over forty years' of Agricultural Department activity. I missed documenting community-level variables, and made most of the usual mistakes.

In retrospect, the quantitative practice of adoption surveys took the most effort and produced the least information of lasting value. Review of the historical documents gave a quite different picture, but was not markedly more cost-effective because of the laborious documentation required (in the days before photocopiers had come into widespread use). Extended personal interviews with farmers coupled with local residence and participant observation (the traditional techniques of anthropology, not employed during the initial survey season) proved quite useful, but the interviewing of key informants selected for their expertise was by far the most cost-effective.

One specific illustration must suffice. Towards the end of three seasons' effort (comprising in all about one year in the field), I interviewed Victor Burke, still in Kenya although retired from the Agriculture Department. When he learned where I had been working,

the quantitative output measures (also drawing upon an immense data base). Trend concludes that the sharply contrasting explanations offered by observers and agency staff did not arise simply because of conflicting, disparate *data bases*. Instead, 'the difficulty lay in conflicting explanations or accounts, each based largely upon a different *kind* of data. The problems we faced involved not only the nature of observational *versus* statistical inferences, but two sets of preferences and biases within the entire research team. The solution was to overturn the existing explanations by offering a third.' (Trend, reprinted in Cook and Reichardt, 1979:83; italics in original).

Triangulation is an important weapon in exposing bias. Obtaining a second expert opinion is an obvious example; but identifying all key stakeholders with an interest in a given matter and interviewing several with widely differing positions is even better. While qualitative enquiry usually does not yield statistically valid samples, the investigator should plan to interview across the range of variation for a given trait or issue. The approach to data is much like that of investigative journalism.

he said (approximately): 'Oh, of course. Those were Leslie Brown's pet farmers. He had them practically eating out of his hand...'.

At the time, I tried to hide my consternation. Not once had any of 'my' farmers mentioned Leslie Brown, perhaps Kenya's most distinguished agricultural officer. I knew from the documents, of course, that he had been in charge of the district; but until that afternoon, I had no inkling that my specific survey area was his favourite (a conclusion quickly verified by other means). Why, then, no mention of his encouragement, no reference to any innovations he promoted?

It then surfaced from further checking among the older farmers and a closer scrutiny of the records that the whole of 'my' area had been resettled after the Mau Mau Emergency (which ended a decade before). An earlier generation of Kikuyu immigrants – labelled as 'Mau Mau' in the 1950s, but previously the District's leading innovators – had been dispossessed of their farms. These were Leslie Brown's 'pet' farmers. The deal struck subsequently between the colonial administration and the Embu was that the Embu would adopt land reform (initially opposed) if the Administration evicted all the Kikuyu who had begun to put down stone houses. The survey respondents answered the questions about their own farming truthfully; they had simply neglected to mention an earlier generation whom they had displaced and from whose practices they learned much.

Assume bias is present, but allow for it by recognizing explicitly a respondents' interests and by cross-checking statements with neutral observers or those holding opposite views.

If studying an institution or field agency, for example, this means gaining access to respondents at all levels and within its various cadres – junior staff as well as managers and professionals. Studies of marketing systems provide another. Questioning both buyers and seller, wholesalers and retailers, about terms of the same transaction (e.g. interest rates on trade credit) often yields an upper and a lower figure. By asking who is lying and why, important insights into relative market power may be gained.

Triangulation in the above cases entails use of more than one method of qualitative enquiry, but may also combine qualitative and quantitative methods to provide complementary information. Used *before* a quantitative survey, for example, qualitative enquiry may help with formulation and pre-testing of questionnaires, since a good questionnaire

Box 5:   Three weeks for preparation of a questionnaire?

I have arranged to 'piggyback' a sociological study on top of a large farm management study which has been collecting its data for a full calendar year. In going to administer the wind-up questionnaire, a one-shot summary being checked with each farmer personally, the senior investigator states that it takes at least three weeks to formulate a good three-page questionnaire.

I say nothing, but privately consider the person a dunderhead. Surely one week, at most. Later, in my own surveys, I discover at great cost that the original estimate was parsimonious. Anticipating answers, insuring common frames of reference, testing items in translation: it can take more than three weeks. And much of this behind the scenes effort must consist of rigorously-pursued qualitative inquiry.

requires comprehensive advanced knowledge about the system being studied, and rigorous preparation (see Boxes 5 and 6). Qualitative enquiry may also generate hypotheses worthy of further investigation, or help to narrow down the questions that more detailed surveys should focus on (Biggs, 1983), though Franzel and Crawford (1988) warn against the assumption that preliminary qualitative enquiry necessarily demands such validation.

Qualitative enquiry may also be useful *after* a formal survey to follow up interesting leads (Fielding and Fielding, 1986). Field staff who are responsible for conducting formal interviews for a quantitative survey invariably acquire many ancillary observations during their enquiry which are not recorded on the official questionnaire. Systematic debriefing may therefore provide as much insight into the subject in question as the questionnaires themselves. Surveys may also help to identify key informants – large landowners, moneylenders or influential traders in a nearby town, for example.

In general, qualitative enquiry after a survey adds depth and context and has particular merit as a research strategy. For policy purposes, however, most is gained by qualitative enquiry in advance of specialized and descriptive studies, to eliminate issues which do not require further study, and identify those which do. Whether used before or after, however, qualitative enquiry helps to establish whether the assumptions made by a given method of quantitative analysis are justified within a given field application.

The problem in any investigative enquiry is that, once recorded, data tend to be taken at face value. It remains true that from a distance one has great difficulty judging if materials are valid simply from internal

Box 6:   Checking the meaning of quantitative questions

We had been using a checklist/questionnaire to evaluate the success of several restocking projects, which had given out goats and sheep to destitute ex-pastoralists in an attempt to help them rejoin the pastoral economy. A key question was the number of small stock necessary to support one family, which is exactly how we posed it to the participants we were interviewing.

It was always possible to get some sort of quantitative estimate: operationally, the question 'worked'. But as the one doing the questioning I could see the item was being interpreted in different ways. What size of family? What composition of the herd by age, sex and species? In good years or bad years? With or without the support of relatives? These might seem small points to the outsider, but for people relying on animals they would dictate different answers and quite a few respondents said so. None of these varying frames of reference would have been evident had we not done the questioning ourselves.

In one area, though, I began to suspect collusion. All respondents gave the same answer, with no variation. Having already received varying answers in two other areas, I thought respondents must have been told the question in advance and perhaps agreed what to answer. But my local translator cleared the matter up at once. In this culture, to get married a man was expected to have a set number of smallstock – a number justified as being what a couple needed to support themselves. Our question had simply tapped a cultural expectation not found in the two areas we had already studied. Hence these answers had both more and less meaning than the others.

evidence (see Box 6). Thus users of qualitative data are often worried that there is no empirical control to prove validity. Triangulation has been the key to resolving this problem within the discipline of anthropology for many years (Naroll 1962), but its role remains undervalued in issue affecting policy research where analysts are less aware of formal procedures to safeguard data quality.

Professionalism
As we emphasized in Part One, qualitative enquiry must be clearly distinguished from informal enquiry. An informal manner, or avoidance of the excessive formality that villagers and farmers often associate with officialdom, is often good tactics when interviewing. But qualitative enquiry, done well, requires as much skill and professionalism as quantitative enquiry; and benefits equally from systematic preparation.

The most obvious cost of failure to plan are wasted journeys. Even relatively short pieces of qualitative enquiry – a series of extended interviews, or a day reading district files – can be enormously expensive in its demands upon time and transport – particularly in countries where fuel is rationed, where military escort is required, and in low population density areas where access to remote areas is restricted by poor roads and heavy rains. Journeys are often wasted through such seemingly trivial omissions as the failure to carry necessary documents, including letters of introduction to local officials and village leaders; or to take into account public holidays, religious festivals, important bureaucratic deadlines (for submission of annual returns, for example) and periods of peak labour demand when officials and farmers have less time for interviewing.

Box 7:   Uncovering bad data

It was a major, multidisciplinary team research report on indigenous agriculture in a part of West Africa which was diverse and interesting. I had visited these areas and written about them, and was delighted to obtain a copy of the report. When enthusiastically recommending it to colleagues from that part of West Africa, however, I noticed several of the most experienced field researchers seemed reluctant to comment. Finally one of them took me aside.

'Didn't you know about their field teams?' he began. Then he explained that there had been a sharp dispute over wages and terms between the field enumerators and the parent research organization. The research institution took the line that its field staff had been recruited from among unemployed school leavers, or had resigned ministry jobs to accept better terms. They would have nowhere else to go. The organization was correct: after some weeks of acrimonious accusations and counter threats, most members of the field interviewing teams went back to work and the larger set of field surveys were brought to completion. 'But I wouldn't trust one piece of evidence those surveys produced', my informant concluded, 'not unless I had firm corroborative evidence. And maybe not even then'.

Inadequate preparation and unwillingness to address problems that emerge when data collection is already underway can also result in monumental writer's block during analysis and report writing. Inexperienced investigators rush into the field and then subsequently discover key topics which were not studied, or serious gaps in their field data. The only way to obtain comparable information across cases – a goal in qualitative work, just as it is in quantitative surveys – is to ensure systematic collection of information about the same points whenever they are relevant.

Advanced planning of qualitative enquiry starts with clear identification of the problems or knowledge gaps that need to be filled. The appropriate combination of methods of enquiry then has to be agreed, taking into account the importance of the problems, the urgency with which decisions are needed and the resources available. The sequence of field work also needs careful consideration, with adequate time available for initial documentation and exploratory enquiry, reviews of progress (if the data collection is to last more than a few weeks), debriefing, and follow-up.

While advanced preparation and planning is important, one advantage of qualitative enquiry is that a greater element of flexibility and learning by doing is possible. As an increasingly detailed and comprehensive picture of the system being studied emerges, extra attention can be given to unresolved issues. Unplanned opportunities providing access to a key informants and documents, the chance to attend important events or visit parallel interventions may also arise that should not be missed. In this respect, qualitative enquiry is more akin to good journalism than to scientific survey sampling. However, pressures to depart from broader plans during fieldwork should be resisted until they become compelling – no field work is completely problem (and pain) free, and the grass often looks temptingly greener on the other side of a methodological fence.

Advanced thinking is also required on how (and at what stage) data is to be enumerated, and how much time will be required for analysis, report writing and outputs. Verbal reporting of key issues may significantly improve timeliness; although some form of written output is in practice usually required as well, and the time required for this is almost always underestimated. As a rule of thumb, it is advisable to allow at least as much time for *thinking* (planning, reviewing, analysing and writing-up) as for actual fieldwork, though for studies on novel problems frequent iteration may blur the distinction between the two.

Retaining and analysing primary documentation is a major problem for qualitative enquiry because of the sheer volume of potential data and its informational richness. It becomes important to anticipate this difficulty in advance, or the investigator can become swamped with partly-analysed materials. Tapes of interviews and documents retain their informational value almost indefinitely, but consist of raw or variable data which must be organized, examined and summarized. Most individual investigators working alone must compromise, recording key interviews in detail but summarizing notes on reports and other data into a framework prepared early in the study.

Another, indeed a key consideration, is *who* should carry out the enquiry. Field work may be carried out quickly by senior staff, more slowly by junior staff, by a specialized consultant (in which case the choice of an appropriate local guide or interpreter may be critical) or a combination of all three. Another aspect of the choice of investigator is the need to achieve the right disciplinary mix – qualitative analysis is generally most productive when it becomes transdisciplinary and holistic. Important public decisions (e.g. approval of a new project, or a policy switch) often face protracted and stringent screening processes, that cover technical, environmental, economic, social, political, legal and institutional aspects. Good work on some of these aspects can be rendered useless if gaps are left in others. Thus, almost by definition, policy-oriented investigation must draw upon multidisciplinary analysis and insights (see Section 3.1).

3.3 Sources of information

This section develops the general arguments of the last section with reflections on the use of important sources of information – documents, field visits, key informants, group discussions, participant observation, team studies, and action research. For more detailed and systematic discussion of the use of these sources within social science research methodology, readers are referred to numerous texts, including: Part 2 of Patton (1980); Chapters 4 and 5 of Patton (1987); Chapters 2 to 4 of Casley and Kumar (1988); Chapter 7 in Salmen (1987); and chapters 2, 3 and 6 in Devereux and Hoddinott (1993).

Documents
Even when allowance is made for searching costs and indifferent quality, a failure to make full use of available material before embarking upon costly data collection is a common fault. There are two problems. The first is to locate relevant published and unpublished documents early. The riposte that no significant sources exist is usually an absurd statement, considering that in addition to the local government and indigenous rural development agencies most low income countries are host to at least a couple of dozen international donors, each with a large appetite for surveys and reports.

Documents there are, even if not perhaps in the obvious places like a library or an information centre. Computer searches are also generally of limited usefulness in locating the unpublished working papers and consultants' reports which have the most policy relevance. Access to such documents may be a problem, though key informants in the capital or provincial headquarters and a formal link with a sponsoring agency usually overcome most of them. International collections, such as those in FAO or the World Bank, and a written enquiry to academics or consultants known to have worked in the area before, are an additional important source.

Having gained access to relevant documents, the next problem is fully to digest the contents. Many documents may include only an occasional relevant paragraph and can be returned quickly. But a good quality technical report may be the product of several principal investigators, working for several months, and may take a whole weekend to digest: picking out the names of relevant contacts who might be worth following up, making copies of crucial sections, gradually building up a mental picture of the systems being studied, assessing the reliability of the source, and identifying important knowledge gaps. The temptation to photocopy and forget is strong, but by the time the photocopy is read it may well be too late!

Field visits

By field visits we refer to a quick official visit to a rural area or project by a consultant or ministry official, often to be met by local project staff and community leaders. They are the form of enquiry that most obviously fit Chambers' (1983) description of rural development tourism; more specifically, being most susceptible to the six traps that he describes:

1. spatial bias – urban, tarmac, roadside;
2. project bias – showpiece villages, success stories;
3. person bias – leaders, men, adopters, progressive farmers;
4. dry season bias – post harvest;
5. diplomatic bias – politeness and timidity;
6. professional bias – disciplinary specialization.

Field visits are often referred to as being informal, but may in fact be highly ritualized social conventions – complete with cavalcades of cars, speeches, visitors books, inspection of buildings, presentation of soft drinks and garlands (see Box 8). If we calculate the total costs of vehicle use, mileage, subsistence claims, per diem, salary costs, and organizing costs, we find that such field visits can be extremely expensive per hour actually spent in the 'field'. Sometimes the entourage has barely arrived before they must be hustled away for various logistical reasons (travel before dark, another village waiting, etc.). Then why do visits at all?

The real purpose of such visits is usually to confer legitimacy upon participants' mutual concerns; to enable a high official or some expert to say he or she has visited the area to hear the concerns of local people or project staff, or to confer legitimacy on a consultants report. Whether anything was actually learned during the visit is almost irrelevant – the event is a form of political theatre.

Where such visits are unavoidable, however, they may nevertheless enable visitors to familiarize themselves with the physical geography of a new area, and to establish useful contacts. Having a visual picture of an area also makes it far to easier to comprehend more complicated and

Box 8:   The formality of informal visits

We get out of the Land Rovers to commence an 'informal' village visit. Chairs are already drawn up in a row before the Party office. Without being told, the villagers correctly identify the important District politician in the group. They begin clapping in unison as he approaches. A welcoming speech is given, then the politician launches into a short speech about seeing that women share in the 'fruits of progress' (this is the 'Year of the Woman').

In the background, women are preparing the fields; it is planting time. The audience of mainly old men and male school leavers claps. Then one steps forward to thank the Party leaders for their wise leadership and to assure everyone present that women in this village are benefiting from Independence.

Warm bottles of Fanta appear and are distributed. The district leaders and expatriates get two each. For some minutes people intermingle. However, there is a rigid social hierarchy underlying our apparent informality. It dictates where people sit, who gives speeches, what was said and even which cars everyone but the expatriate rides in.

As we ride away, I ask the Agricultural Officer why he is so glum. This is his visit, he explains, charged against his Department's vote. Now he will have no petrol for any real fieldwork until next month's allocation.

subtle written materials and discussion about an area. Almost any form of travel is better than none.

Furthermore, there are many ways in which short field visits can be made more useful at little extra cost. More careful selection of fewer stopping off points, giving more time at each, can result in a significant increase in meaningful hours of contact (once inevitable formalities have been dispensed with), including more opportunities to make small yet often revealing departures from convention. More overnight stops allow visitors to spend time talking with villagers, and create opportunities for extended evening discussions in a less formal atmosphere with local staff, when the party retires (as it usually does) to the local government guest house.

The large chunks of time spent travelling may also be made more productive. Experienced investigators arrange for key informants from the area to accompany them, even perhaps rotating between several such temporary assistants during one trip. Itineraries can also be planned to ensure that they take in the full agro-ecological diversity of the area.

If freed from the anxiety of being 'found out', local staff can also do much to make official field visits more productive, even without offending local leaders. Visits can be used as a pretext for bringing together representatives or leaders from throughout the project area who rarely get a chance to meet as a group; with the most important discussion invariably taking place before the visitors arrive and after they leave! Formal greetings can be cut down in length, to allow the party to divide into smaller groups for informal discussion, longer tours of the village and its surrounds and more systematic PRA activities (for examples from Zimbabwe, see Harvey et al., 1987).

Alternatively visits can be linked in with project monitoring, providing a chance for junior staff to describe operational problems, and for senior staff to balance quantitative performance indicators against qualitative factors including staff calibre. Much depends, however, upon the extent to which organizational culture permits open exchange between superiors and their juniors. Heginbottom (1975), for example, describes how field visits can degenerate into ritual 'dressings down' of junior staff who have failed (perhaps for very good reasons) to meet targets.

In sum, the line between sterile rural development tourism and productive qualitative enquiry is thin, and with a little imagination, forethought and skill it can be breached easily. What Harvey et al., (1987) say applies to field visits generally:

> The most valuable RRA techniques were judged to be self-imposed discipline, the use of checklists, careful organization and the use of existing information before visiting the schemes.

Official field visits by outsiders often include a series of more or less stage-managed visits to farms. While making due allowance for the fact that even a series of such visits may fail to cover the range of diversity among farmers, such visits may nevertheless be extremely insightful – though they are also demanding on the investigator. We have both found that an initial 'farm walk' is helpful to gain a quick overview of enterprises and to create less confrontational opportunities for discussion, which may lead to insights that can then be explored in more depth back at the farmer's compound. This initial period is when farmers are judging their visitor, too. It is important to be as well informed in advance as possible, so as to be able to ask reasonably astute questions. For this reason the most valuable informants are best left until later in an enquiry when the investigator can make the best use of a limited exposure.

Once again, any outside investigator (whether expatriate or national) needs to be properly introduced by someone the farmers being visited know and trust. Good translation as one moves about is vital. For extended interviews, farmers must be warned in advance; one will be lucky to average more than three to four in a day, though this obviously depends upon many factors.

Every third or fourth day should be spent writing out detailed notes and preparing for the next round of interviews. The techniques for a survey with pre-set questionnaires are, of course, somewhat different from those described here and are well outlined in the standard texts (Casley and Kumar, 1988; O'Barr *et al.*, 1973; Hursh-Cesar and Roy, 1976; Devereux and Hoddinott, 1993; and Fowler, 1993).

Key informants

Perhaps the single most important diagnostic feature of good qualitative enquiry is its full exploitation of insights from key informants. By key informants we mean persons whose position or previous experience gives them particularly valuable information on a given topic. If the basis is *position*, the key informant becomes in effect a surrogate observer for the investigator. On the other hand, if the basis is *experience*, the informant provides the investigator with a chance to view information from other sources in historical perspective – in effect a longitudinal 'time slice'.

Key informants should not be seen as a low-cost alternative for a representative sample of the population, for they are of interest precisely because they depart from the average and usual (see Box 9). Rather, their special position or experience gives them unique insights that may yield a very high return to the investigator's time.

Researchers differ in the opinion on how formal interviews with key informants should be, and this obviously depends upon subject matter and cultural context. Most writers favour at least semi-structuring of interviews, through reference to a checklist of key questions or issues that need to be covered, e.g. McCracken (1988:24); McCracken, Pretty and Conway (1988:20). However, informants must be given a free rein to raise unexpected topics; and care is required to avoid leading questions.

Other investigators feel it is intrusive to refer to, or to take notes, which may affect what people are willing to reveal. Questions, they argue, can easily be memorized, and it is possible to produce remarkably detailed notes on an interview by recall if this is done within a few hours. However, when the conversation is allowed to flow freely it is easy to omit important questions and prompts, and some form of simultaneous note-taking becomes essential when names, detailed facts or numerical information is provided. Even in quite remote areas most people are now familiar with clipboards, questionnaires and even cassette recorders, and do not object to their being used so long as they are asked in advance, and given adequate assurances about confidentiality.

Often the best way to combine methodological discipline with a friendly manner is to conduct interviews in pairs, with one person taking notes

Box 9:   The yam grower

We were nearing the end of a parallel farm interview, which I was conducting with a local interpreter to cross-check the findings of the larger, quantitative survey. The farmer, an old woman, asks if, now that my questions are finished, may she tell me about yam growing? She explains that this is her speciality and soon she will die. It is important knowledge for a poor woman like herself, because yams give a high return to effort and require little land (both true), but the Agriculture Department doesn't know about yams (also then true).

She proceeds to give me some twenty minutes of detailed instructions: about soils, varieties and yam husbandry. We tape what she says, but because I know nothing whatever about yams or yam growing (a crop not even on my questionnaire), all the technical details are lost on me.

I later try to interest the Agriculture Department in the woman's yam growing observation. They tell me yams are not in their official programme. To this day I wonder what empirical observations that patient old woman was trying to pass on to her posterity. She certainly gave every impression of knowing a great deal about yams and was acknowledged locally as an authority on that topic (according to my assistant). Perhaps he listened and something of her experience survives?

and checking that nothing is omitted, while the other asks the questions. When interviews are conducted through an interpreter this is a necessity, and note-taking keeps the investigator busy (and awake!) while the interpreter or field assistant is trying to clarify questions and answers in the local language. Considerable trust and mutual understanding is needed between the two; for the investigator can easily become impatient if he or she feels excluded from much of the conversation, while the interpreter can quickly become irritated if persistently urged to translate before having clarified exactly what the informant is saying.

Group meetings
Where a rural development project operates through community-level groups, semi-formal meetings between group members and staff are an important form of information exchange. Communication at such meetings is greatly complicated by the need for any speaker to take into account not only how other locals as well as outsiders interpret what they say. This is why such meetings are often quite superficial and unhelpful to all concerned (see Box 9).

However, a little bit of advanced planning can help. Participants should be clear who outsiders are, and what their interest in visiting them is; a list of specific topics or issues to cover may help. If so, then it may be possible for a local staff member to introduce and lead them, directing attention away from visitors and reducing the stultifying delays associated with translation. It is also generally more productive to split large and diverse groups into smaller 'focus groups' of people with common interests (e.g. men, women and youth; labourers and owner-occupiers etc). This not only gives more people a chance to speak, but provides opportunities for triangulation.

Participant observation
Participant observation is the technique most closely associated with anthropologists, whose classical method was to take up residence in an area and to share its daily life over a year or more. This exposure affords the time needed to learn the local language and to observe an area's daily life and farming calendar. Such intensive field work is required to understand and explain the cognitive elements in behaviour, to identify cultural norms and expectations, and to describe in detail how livelihood is organized. Therefore, access to a carefully compiled ethnography (i.e. a detailed and holistic description of a society) can be quite valuable in explaining behaviour and activities that otherwise seem inexplicable to the outsider. Studies which illustrate the practical usefulness of anthropological enquiry at its best include: Moran (1981) on settlement in the Amazon; Eder (1982) on economic success in the rural Philippines; Greenwood (1976) on the collapse of commercial agriculture in a Spanish Basque town; Dahl (1979) on Boran pastoralism in northern Kenya; Barlett (1980) on decisionmaking; Galaty *et al.* (1981) on the future of Africa's pastoralists, and Colson (1971) and Scudder (1982) on the social effects of resettlement.

In attenuated form some aspects of participant observation can also contribute to evaluation studies. One of us gained invaluable insights into indebtedness and credit in India, by getting heavily into debt while writing up back in the UK! It is often possible to arrange to 'tag along' as a participant, say, in a farmer training course; to follow a new recruit through the steps needed in becoming an irrigation scheme tenant; or spend a day doing the rounds with an extension officer (Moris, 1981). For examples of using participant observation to evaluate World Bank projects, see Salmen (1987), including methodological hints. Participant observation on such occasions can tell an experienced analyst many things which would not otherwise be learned. For example, in East Africa, farmers on official courses are often treated as if they are primary school students – sitting on the same benches and being lectured at in the same tone of voice.

Team studies

Team studies and short multidisciplinary field workshops are a relatively new technique in rural enquiry, associated particularly with FSR. There are two leading versions:

1. use of site-based field seminar/training to identify local problems (Peuse and Mbaga, 1987);
2. the placement of a multi-disciplinary field team in an area to conduct a preliminary 6–10 day survey, or *sondeo* (Hildebrand, 1981).

The terms workshop, seminar and field study all indicate the basic intention, that a group of people jointly examine a situation and try to arrive at a better understanding of local constraints, options for improvement and priorities of action. Such events create opportunities for intensive interaction between people who share an interest in a common issue or topic, but do not normally have much contact – not just scientists from different disciplines, but also policymakers, ministry officials, local extension workers, community leaders and farmers themselves. Workshops are typically very intensive, going all day and into each evening for several days. A sense of collective responsibility to analyse problems jointly and holistically, and to write a common report is easier to maintain if all participants live and eat together during the workshop.

Team members may fan out to conduct on-farm interviews each day (preferably in multi-disciplinary pairs, as in Hildebrand's *sondeo*), meeting as a group to discuss findings in the evening. Alternatively, the whole team decamps to a village for group interviews and exchange of views over a day or more. A third possibility is to bring villagers and their leaders into a central base, perhaps a local farmers' training centre, as part of a joint exploratory seminar. In all cases, having too many people involved reduces effectiveness and multiplies logistic problems.

Less commonly, a field group may try to carry out an extended survey utilizing conventional questionnaires. However, this rapidly becomes expensive and sacrifices the particular advantages the assembly offers for interdisciplinary and intergroup communication and problem analysis. Closer to the mark is Hildebrand's suggestion that the field team reworks and refines its analysis as it goes, through a *successive approximation* approach drawing upon rapid, qualitative sources to refine a collectively-constructed analysis of local problems. The full potential of the approach probably also requires that those questioned are themselves part of the group and share in defining the problems and solutions (Reason, 1988).

Action research

By action research we refer to activities or interventions intended to achieve tangible (though perhaps vaguely defined) development goals, while at the same time increasing our understanding of how (i.e. by what combination of inputs, decisions and activities) those goals can be achieved. Perhaps the most established form of action research is the execution of on-farm trials and experiments. Tangible goals here consist of increased output or profitability, while the research goal is improved understanding of the relationship between inputs, agronomic practices and crop output. Note that use of the word *trial* generally implies that the dominant form of analysis is quantitative, whereas the word *experiment* in this context implies that evaluation is primarily qualitative, or based on the participants' own direct observation. However, the distinction is a blurred one, since the qualitative lessons learnt through trials may be as important as the formal trial results (see Section 4.1.2). Additionally, Lightfoot and Barker (1988) warn that 'farmer managed' trials often provide unsatisfactory data and inconclusive results.

Action research is not, however, confined to agricultural research. It has been particularly important in validating and refining highly innovatory activities. Useful examples include: the early development of agroforestry in Kenya by the Mazingira institute (see Buck in Wellard and Copestake, forthcoming); and the transfer of water-lifting technology by Proshika to groups of landless or near landless labourers in Bangladesh (see Wood and Palmer-Jones, 1991). In both instances complex technical and social decisions had to be made: what trees to grow, how best to organize community tree nurseries, in the Kenyan case; under what conditions pump ownership would be profitable, and how best to organize pump-owning groups, in the Bangladesh case. Note also that both projects were initiated by NGOs, and involved a high level of collaboration between agency staff and villagers.

As in the case of on-farm research these action research projects were subject to both quantitative and qualitative enquiry. Wood and Palmer-Jones describe the considerable difficulties encountered in trying to secure accurate survey data through field staff who were already overburdened with operational tasks, and also overwhelmed on a number of occasions during the project by serious flooding and ensuing relief work. Buck, on the other hand, emphasizes the qualitative nature of information flowing from the agroforestry project and its rapid dissemination through informal NGO networks. We can conclude that the full benefits of an action research can generally only be realized through some form of systematic documentation, both qualitative and quantitative – but in practice often completely lacking.

3.4 Conclusion: some key concepts

We can identify certain common themes from this chapter which tend to distinguish qualitative from quantitative forms of enquiry when used in a development context. Specifically, we shall argue that qualitative approaches require intelligence rather than applied research; indicators rather than measured coefficients; and key informants rather than respondents.

Intelligence rather than applied research

Most rural development planners have some training in scientific methods and some acquaintance with either field surveys or scientific experiments. Again and again analysts call for more and better applied research as the means to supply the data needed for planning rural interventions. Furthermore, thousands of field studies have been justified because of their purported contributions to development, just as in many other instances the lack of relevant information has been used to justify inaction or failure.

However, is more applied research the answer? Some studies by sociologists (Scott and Shore, 1979) as well as policy analysts themselves (Patton and Sawicki, 1986; House and Shull, 1991) suggest that much 'policy research' is either inappropriate, inconclusive, or too slow. Chambers (1983) certainly suggested as much when criticizing the mainly negative role 'academics' have played within rural development to date.

If we turn to comparable situations in the political, military and business fields, we find that decisionmakers usually act without having access to high quality applied research. Because of strategic concerns, they routinely organize the intelligence at hand (whatever its source) and then proceed to act upon their assessments of the most likely situation. What they produce in order to take decisions is orderly and systematic, but not scientific: hence the designation intelligence rather than applied research. There are at least three key differences: they draw upon multiple sources of varying quality; they judge information not only by its content ('face validity') but also in terms of the credibility of its source; and, finally, they adjust the depth of the information-gathering effort to suit changing strategic concerns. We suggest that in all three respects, organizing data for planning purposes is more like intelligence work than it is applied research (here see the discussion in Dedijer and Jequier, 1987). In qualitative enquiry, a great deal rests upon the analyst's own judgement about sources, whereas in scientific work the adequacy of one's methods provides certainty about data quality.

Indicators rather than coefficients

In systems that are well understood, analysts know what to measure. Inputs and outputs are represented in the form of rigorously-obtained parametric statistics, which in turn become production coefficients when analysing how the system performs. Anyone used to employing such data comes to expect them automatically. The rural development literature abounds with spurious but apparently rigorous coefficients: income per annum, yields per hectare, calorific intake per day, water demand per plant, and so forth. Most are associated with 'hard science' models portraying, we must assume, the activities of real households, farms, plants and animals.

In real world situations, however, actual measurements are often not yet available. In their place, the analyst substitutes coefficients derived elsewhere: some from the general literature, some from similar areas of the country, and a few perhaps from past experience. Thus in many cases the apparent rigor of calculations is misleading. While actual circumstances may, indeed, fall within the predicted range we have no firm scientific reason for assuming they do; except the faith that the local system resembles better studied examples elsewhere.

Qualitative enquiry assumes instead we either do not have powerful measurements or else we do not understand a complex situation sufficiently to interpret how components systems behave. Instead we try to identify key indicators (either quantitative or qualitative) which on an experiential basis we can judge have clear cut meaning. For example (see Box 4), when judging the impact on pastoral households of a drought, the conventional approach requires an array of production coefficients: rates of mortality of different classes of livestock, the degree of depletion of key forage resources, the status of household savings, and so forth. Obviously, we know how to make such assessments: an experienced range scientist could lead a team into the field and with a month's effort tell us the extent and severity of drought. It takes this much time because when measuring production coefficients they must *all* be present; absence of data on any key variable renders the whole exercise pointless.

A qualitative approach will instead focus upon certain crucial indicators, such as the atypical sale of young breeding stock, to signal a change in system status (to use the scientist's jargon). In the Maasai drought case reported in Box 10, it was the marketing specialist's prior experience with Maasai stock sellers which led to his conclusion. Under most conditions, Maasai herd owners retain their female stock to build up herd sizes. They would be loathe to risk such valuable immature animals by trekking them long distances to market. When this behavioural change was observed, the analyst concludes something significant is taking place which merits further scrutiny. Thus, the collaborative observations from three 'fuzzy' sources, all obtained qualitatively, gave a more firm result than might have been obtained from a major data collecting exercise of a conventional nature.

Box 10:   Deciding when a drought has begun

The project team had reported that a major drought appeared to be starting. However, during the half day they had available to verify this fact, two external experts saw only tall grass and fat cows. Now, on my next visit to Dar es Salaam, I am called to task by the Embassy's economic officer. He says we have been making up the crisis to obtain funds from Washington. First, the external visitors saw no drought. Second, satellite imagery seems to indicate only normal conditions for a typical dry season. Third, the government's rainfall statistics show average distributions. Unless we can give hard figures on numbers of cattle dying monthly and on percentages of stressed families, he cannot support our conclusion that a crisis situation is developing.

I answer that we, too, have several sources of admittedly 'fuzzy'information. First, the marketing officer reports that Maasai are bringing immature females for sale into distant markets (both unusual events), which means they fear young animals will die as the season progresses. Second, the veterinarian tells us the mature stock being brought to other markets are in poor condition, have been trekked long distances, and are coming in greater numbers. Third, we learn that Maasai stock owners are moving herds into the better-watered, tsetse bush where many cattle will die from disease. Taken together, these qualitative indicators support what the Maasai themselves are saying, that a major drought has begun.

In retrospect, the Maasai were correct. While there had been average rainfall, its spotty distribution left many areas without enough grass, and many cattle eventually died throughout South Maasailand. But we never were able to document this fact with precise figures.

Key informants rather than respondents

A further difference between qualitative and quantitative enquiry exists with regard to how 'respondents' are regarded. In the typical socio-economic survey, a respondent is treated as the *object* of study. Information recorded carries value for analysts because it was acquired as part of a sampling plan, and hence can be aggregated into a composite statistical picture. We do not expect to take much interest in the holder of the information as an individual. The validity of survey results depends crucially upon adhering to the sampling plan and carefully standardizing all responses to insure they are 'objective'.

Throughout these pages we instead lean towards seeing a respondent as the *subject* of research, what anthropologists call a 'key informant'.

Doing so turns the usual research procedures upside-down. What to the quantitative analyst may seem merely 'anecdotal' and 'incidental' information to the qualitative enquirer becomes critical data because of the value of the source. For example, in Box 10 the nearly silent contributors are the Maasai stockowners themselves. They, of all people, know their own environment and have an interest in accurately predicting whether a drought is beginning to occur. If we view them as they would be seen from an intelligence operative's standpoint, they become the very best sources one could desire. However, to use such sources the analyst must probe and compare: about which areas are Maasai herd owners speaking? How recently have they seen field conditions? Whom have they talked to? How does this season compare with earlier ones they have experienced? These are not questions an interviewer would ask when obtaining questionnaire responses, but they are vital if the analyst must weigh each response according to the credibility of its source. We know from military intelligence that such methods work, and can yield reliable conclusions; what we need to recognize is that they do not derive from the same procedures which a quantitative survey would employ.

4 The Application of Qualitative Enquiry

THIS SECTION of the paper returns to some specific areas of demand for rural information (introduced in Part Two), and how qualitative enquiry can help to meet them. It then considers the constraints to increased and better use of qualitative enquiry, and how they can be overcome.

The pluralist approach to rural enquiry that we have advocated restrains us from being overly prescriptive, for the appropriate combination of methods will vary according to context. However, some indication as to which methods might be appropriate to particular subjects is probably helpful, even if highly selective.

4.1 Agricultural research and technology development

Given that agriculture is the mainstay of the economy in rural areas, and that the introduction of new technology has proved a particularly powerful way of inducing change in production and incomes, the domain of agricultural research and technology development merits particular attention. It is probably no coincidence that it is also an area in which the debate over appropriate methodology has been particularly lively.

Following Chambers and Jiggins (1987), this section outlines three broad traditions of enquiry within the domain of agricultural research policy that currently coexist – often uncomfortably.

1. The orthodox scientific tradition, closely associated with the *transfer of technology* (TOT) model of agricultural innovation, is the most firmly rooted of the three. Arnon (1989) is perhaps the most comprehensive recent review.
2. *Farming systems research* (FSR), is the best generic label for a cluster of rival approaches, all quite similar (in their emphasis on adaptive and on-farm research, for example), but employing diverse acronyms (FSR and D, FSR/E, OFR, OFCOR etc.). Useful introductions to FSR include Hildebrand (1981), Simmonds (1985) and Shaner *et al.* (1982).
3. *Farmer participatory research* (FPR), also referred to as *farmer first and last* (FFL), departs from FSR in proposing much greater farmer

involvement in all stages of agricultural research and technology development, and stressing the importance of indigenous technical knowledge. Useful references include Farrington and Martin (1987), Farrington (1988), and Chambers, Pacey and Thrupp (1989).

The transfer of technology model

The dominant approach within the orthodox sciences, or what Kuhn (1970) referred to as normal science – is to divide reality into segments which each discipline probes independently. In the field of agricultural research, scientists divide agriculture both into disciplines or components (botany, soil science, entomology, agronomy etc.), and into enterprizes (maize, wheat, dairying, cattle, forestry etc.). The next step is to replicate each enterprise on the research station and identify ways of improving productivity through experimentation according to the canons of scientific method. Technical advances are then reintroduced to farmers through extension services and the media.

Outside the research station itself, rural enquiry within this tradition has chiefly served to establish which crops should receive priority, and to investigate the gap between the practices and performance of research station and farmers. Methods of enquiry, until recently, tended to consist of an uneasy combination of highly formal quantitative statistical surveys, and informal personal contacts between individual scientists and farmer associates.

Much research under this tradition has tended to follow individual whims or intuitions of researchers themselves, or to be driven by the vague 'modernist' supposition that by combining better varieties with high inputs it is possible to achieve spectacular yield breakthroughs. Many scientists have also assumed that basic research naturally precedes applied research, and that technology development flows automatically from unconstrained natural science enquiry.

This is of course one strategy, and it has paid off handsomely, particularly in the irrigated wheat and paddy fields of Asia. However, success has not been universal: greatest in areas with stable environments, a high degree of commercialization and crop specialization; but lowest in poor, drought-prone, remote and highly diverse regions dominated by (semi-subsistence) smallholder production. In other words, orthodox agricultural research has been most successful in areas where the difference between prevailing farming systems and research station plots are smallest. We shall follow the tradition of referring to these 'difficult' regions as 'complex, diverse and risky' (CDR) – see Chapter 3 in Kesseba (1989) and the introduction to Chambers *et al.* (1989), for example. Even within 'privileged' areas where TOT seems most applicable, a strong case can be made to broaden coverage to include 'soft science' and 'soft models' – here see Wilson and Morren (1990).

Indeed, Wilson and Morren's book makes many of the same points we stress here, but in the context of conventional scientific research.

Farming systems research

Farming systems research (FSR) developed simultaneously in different countries through efforts to identify alternative strategies that were more appropriate to the needs of smallholder farming systems in CDR regions. Pioneers included Hildebrand in Guatemala, Norman in Nigeria, Collinson in East Africa, and Rhoades in Peru. They were united by a commitment to arriving at a better understanding of how existing smallholder systems actually worked in order to identify key production constraints. This required that field enquiry began with an open and holistic approach, free of any presuppositions that existing systems were in any way inferior or unscientific.

This inclination to start with detailed investigation of what existing systems actually are, rather than how they might be, runs counter to the dominant TOT model described above, and has encountered resistance. Partly, the problem has been psychological, arising from the need for professional or intellectual reversals (Chambers, 1983): from 'telling' farmers to listening to them; and from a reductionist to a holistic perspective. But it is also institutional/political, for to let systematic analysis of existing farming systems influence research priorities requires reform of resource allocation and decisionmaking structures based on scientific disciplines or particular crops. Thus the previous failure to cope with the problems of complex farming systems has in part been intrinsic to the way many scientists organize their own work (Maxwell, 1984a; Collinson, 1987). Fixation with the TOT approach has also kept researchers locked into an unproductive sequence of investigatory tasks partitioned into the various natural science disciplines, and encouraged a mind-set that pays little genuine attention to context, except as a constraint on adoption (Belshaw and Hall, 1972; Wilson and Morren, 1990).

The case for a deeper understanding of diverse local contexts, for relating agricultural research more closely to established and proven local technology, and for strengthening evaluation and dissemination of findings is virtually unanswerable at a theoretical level. It was accepted in several of the international agricultural research centres even before those promoting FSR had a clear idea how to achieve their aims in practice.

Different centres then devoted much energy to developing their own models and procedures for FSR, generally including:

O classification of farmers into recommendation domains or target groups with relatively homogenous farming systems;

o diagnosis of key constraints within each farming system;
o development of detailed recommendations through experimentation, including on-farm trials, for each category or zone;
o evaluation of proposed interventions against the criterion of whole farm/household situation;
o verification or results, often with farmer participation;
o dissemination through extension services;
o evaluation by means of rates of adoption.

Section 3.1 has already acknowledged the boost that this work – particularly emphasis on the need for more systematic diagnosis – gave to the application of qualitative methods of enquiry, and to the development of rapid rural appraisal (see Chapter 3, Wilson and Morren, 1990). FSR also strengthened the role of economists in research evaluation, helping to ensure that technical packages were more carefully and realistically costed (Simmonds, 1985).

However, refining FSR procedures took time, and mistakes were made. It was understandable that farming systems researchers sought to achieve rigour and scientific respectability through widespread use of detailed quantitative surveys or expensive multidisciplinary studies; but the cost and time required for such surveys also provided ammunition for defenders of the orthodox approach. At ILCA, for example, 'adopting' FSR initially meant establishing zonal research teams with a multidisciplinary composition. The lengthy systems descriptions produced for each zone have been of little apparent benefit to ILCA's ongoing research programme.

The early record with respect to incorporating FSR findings into formal results, usually by means of elaborate and expensive field surveys and dispersed experiments was no better. Lightfoot and Barker (1988) concluded from a postal questionnaire of 41 on-farm research practitioners that 'many if not most farming systems research projects fail to provide useful information to farmers or to station-based researchers'. Many station-based scientists would agree. For example, while most CGIAR centres *claim* to have adopted some form of FSR, in reality few give it prominence. ILCA, for example, which had the largest commitment has largely returned to orthodox component research, while paying lip service to FSR by suggesting that the initial phase of work is now no longer necessary. Most of the numerous, and highly diverse, USAID projects that adopted the FSR label without having a clear idea what this entailed, also made only limited headway in integrating FSR into mainstream research.

The underlying need for strengthening agricultural research appropriate to the needs of smallholders in CDR regions, therefore remains, along with the associated problem of how to handle such complexity and diversity. Neither is the problem confined to natural science and economics, for ideally innovations should be screened with regard to environmental, social, political, institutional and even legal/ethical criteria (as in the case of biotechnology, for example). Clearly it would be too expensive and unwieldy to achieve this by adding further screening stages, or gates, each controlled by a different discipline. Thus the need for adopting a more holistic, interdisciplinary approach remains compelling – however difficult it is to implement within the present structure of professional disciplines.

If looking at all the components by conventional means across an entire farming systems is not feasible, what are the alternatives? The key task is the early diagnosis of key problems and promising lines of enquiry (see Box 11). Finding and developing an initial lead requires information, but not necessarily in a highly standardized and scientific form – what Keller (1990) terms 'opportunity analysis'. Those searching for strategies will review (and perhaps discard) many options as they rapidly acquire a limited amount of raw information about many aspects of the system. Then, as certain constraints and solutions come to the forefront, these will be subjected to more searching enquiry and (eventually) to systematic testing. Occasional instances where trans-disciplinary insights have emerged – Zandstra et al. (1979) on risk management in Columbia peasant farming and Norman, et al. (1982) on northern Nigerian land-use systems, for example – suggest that it is possible.

This brings us back to the question of qualitative enquiry as potentially the most effective approach for securing rapid feedback about local constraints, and the attractiveness of proposed solutions. The place for more systematic quantitative work comes later, in refining and validating an initial proposal.

Armed with this insight it is now worth reviewing some of the established FSR techniques. The *sondeo*, developed by Hildebrand and his ICTA colleagues (a multi-disciplinary team staying in a given area from 6–10 days) seems to be particularly suitable. It is perhaps no coincidence that the intensive team visit is also a key weapon in the armoury of rapid participatory appraisal discussed in Section 3.1. *Yield gap* analysis, as developed at IRRI in the Philippines by Herdt and his colleagues is directed at the same problem and may perhaps be equally effective in different contexts, despite having developed into a highly quantitative approach wedded to conventional farm economics (see Chapters 8 and 12 in Cernea, Coulter and Russell, 1985).

However, FSR has come to rely increasingly upon so-called informal diagnostic surveys or farm visits as its initial exploratory tool for looking at a given system in particular communities. For example, CIMMYT in East Africa has emphasized short diagnostic surveys, with stress on the single-visit farm interview which Collinson himself pioneered in Tanzania's Sukumaland (Collinson, 1972).

Box 11:   Orthodox agricultural research – validating hunches

During a review of ILCA's field research and zonal programmes in 1986 the two which appeared to me to have any sense of direction were those where a promising line of attack had been located early: alley cropping and fodder banks. Once scientists found something which met genuine local needs, work went ahead rapidly on a broad front to refine an implementation package (here requiring co-operation from those knowing economics, politics and land tenure) while the necessary basic research was done to understand the technical components more fully.

I suspect *most* agricultural innovations are derived in this fashion, starting with a lucky hunch which can be tested among a circle of co-operating farmers, and then followed up with systematic work once it seems that it does offer an attractive farm-level pay-off. If so, then a key problem is finding a mechanism for generating the initial hunches.

Note that in the two ILCA examples it wasn't the scientific properties of *Stylo* as a grass or of the alley cropping species which suggested the line of attack. Both innovations consisted of institutional re-arrangements which fitted into evolving farming systems. The role of orthodox scientific research was then clear – to deepen technical understanding, refine the initial insight and confirm its viability.

What one immediately discovers in such fieldwork is that short diagnostic surveys do not allow for the full exploration of many topics on the same farm. They also must take at face value farmers' own reports about dates, quantities, prices and areas. The limitation of the amount of time which any one farmer can give to the diagnostic effort dictates a severe prioritizing of questioning to the critical aspects. By way of contrast, the *sondeo* uses a multidisciplinary team whose internal discussions build up a jointly acquired picture of the locality during the reconnaissance itself. Collinson's single visit questionnaires, on the other hand, are perhaps only successful in the hand of quite experienced investigators.

We have emphasized the importance of qualitative enquiry in diagnosis. However it may also play a useful role at other stages of FSR, such as specifying exactly what farmers' key goals are (yield per acre, reduced labour, greater food security etc.), or suggesting recommendation domains on the basis of economic and sociological as well as agroecological criteria (Wotowiec *et al.*, 1988). Qualitative enquiry based on the maintenance of a diary or note-book, can be extremely important in on-farm trials, sometimes providing more interesting information than the formal trial results (Tripp, 1982; Sutherland, 1987). Where farming systems are changing rapidly as in areas of new settlement, time delays undermine usefulness of a strict cycle of diagnosis, testing and validation. One remedy for this is to base rural enquiry on carefully-selected casestudy farmers whose activities and responses to different technology options can be monitored continuously (Maxwell, 1984b and 1984c; Yin, 1984).

Even where farming systems are not subject to rapid change, overcomplicated and formal processes of data collection can easily undermine farming systems research. Having embraced it reluctantly, some government and donor agencies have then smothered it with bureaucratic constraints, and complained about its lack of cost-effectiveness! Baker (1992), for example, argues that by focusing on adaptation of technology, crucial institutional and policy variables have been systematically excluded from consideration. He argues for a reintegration of farming systems research with broader research into policy and agrarian change, in part through 'renewed commitment to in-depth household and village studies' (see also Berdegué, 1992; and Bebbington in Booth, 1992).

Farmer participatory research
Our first conclusion, then, is that considerable scope remains for improvement in both orthodox and farming systems approaches to agricultural research through the more imaginative and flexible application of methods of qualitative enquiry. Farmer participatory research (FPR) represents a more far-reaching response to the limited effectiveness of FSR in CDR regions (see Rhoades, 1982, 1984, 1985; Bunch, 1985; Richards, 1985; Conway, 1985; McCracken, Pretty and Conway, 1988; Farrington and Martin, 1988; and Chambers, Pacey and Thrupp, 1989). In brief, its proponents accepted the need for more systematic enquiry into existing farming systems, but have concluded that this is not enough. They argue that the balance of experience and knowledge about agriculture in these regions dictates that local farmers should not just be consulted, but should *actively participate* in the planning and execution of research.

The emergence of FPR out of FSR, and of Participatory Rural Appraisal (PRA) out of RRA (see Section 3.1) are clearly closely related. Additional influences on which FPR has drawn are the social science literature on empowerment and the broader tradition of action research (see Sections 3.1 and 3.3 respectively). However, a further insight into the origin of FPR can be derived from our discussion of strategies for handling information within decisionmaking bureaucracies, namely that when the complexity of relevant information (arising in this case from a high level of diversity) becomes too great to be handled by senior decisionmakers, delegation and decentralization is a logical response.

Farmer participatory research is a relatively young idea, and the extent to which it should be seen as complementary to orthodox and FSR approaches (and if so in what ways) or as a radical alternative to them is still much debated. Some advocates combine advocacy of FPR, with a bias towards low input or organic farming techniques of farming, and ideological hostility towards what we may (for want of a better phrase) refer to as the modernist research/agribusiness complex.

Others, on the other hand, (Farrington and Martin, 1988, for example) view FPR as a mechanism by which farmers can exert a stronger 'demand-pull' on research and technology development; raising more fundamental questions about the relative influence of technocratic enquiry (whether qualitative or quantitative), and political pressure (and even consumer sovereignty) on policy.

4.2 Other spheres of activity

The project cycle
The 'projectization' of rural development is a phenomenon that has been particularly associated with international donors, and bureaucratic pressures have resulted in the elaboration of increasingly complicated guidelines. Rondonelli (1983), for example, divides the project cycle into nearly fifty distinct stages. However, the charge of excessive procedural complexity (see also FAO, 1986) is only one of several basic criticisms that can be made of the dominance of the project cycle. Uphoff (1990:1402) considers the five main weaknesses of the project approach to have been:

1. excessive size and complexity, based upon the unproven assumption that there are always economies of scale;
2. cost-based monitoring, excessive preoccupation with spending agreed sums of finance, partially because staff are assessed in large measure by their ability to spend up to budget, but more fundamentally because high levels of expenditure on administration and project supervision can only be justified by high levels of project spending;
3. limited time-horizons, imposed on projects by the often arbitrary project life;
4. a blueprint approach, leaving little scope for redesigning the project and 'learning-by-doing';
5. unilateralism, – so-called project 'beneficiaries' are given little scope for influencing project design and implementation (see also Hoare and Crouch, 1988).

74

A sixth factor which we would add is:

6. a bias towards measurable goals, on the grounds of bureaucratic convenience (Braun, 1991:314).

From our information-systems perspective, all these limitations can be seen in part as weaknesses in the mechanisms for packaging or screening relevant information so as to enable key decisions to be made by relatively few people. Two extreme ways of reducing this problem can then be distinguished:

○ to decentralize or delegate; or
○ (in the absence of institutional reform) to find more efficient ways of channelling and screening relevant information.

The first option requires a commitment within donor agencies to projects that are smaller, longer, more flexible and more participatory. To emphasize that such reforms represent a radical departure from traditional projects, advocates of such changes have labelled them anti-projects (Chambers, 1987; Braun, 1991), or para-projects (Uphoff, 1991).

Given the pressures for public accountability, not to mention the bureaucratic convenience of large projects, there is little prospect of achieving such radical reform very quickly. Meanwhile, qualitative enquiry, as we have already seen, offers a range of methods for improving the quality of information flow within existing decision-making structures. Molnar (1989:10) outlines eight points at which RRA can be incorporated usefully into the project cycle; while Harvey *et al.* (1987) provide a useful case-study of RRA use within a conventional (i.e. highly centralized) irrigation rehabilitation project. An incremental approach to improving the project cycle may also have more radical long-term implications, since consultation with clients and intended beneficiaries may also encourage their subsequent participation in decisionmaking.

One final question on the project cycle that needs to be addressed is the relationship between qualitative enquiry and the logical framework, originally developed for USAID in the 1960s (and since adopted in one form or another by most official donors and many NGOs). The basic framework is depicted in Table 8, and described in detail by Coleman (1987).

With its emphasis on the need for *objectively verifiable indicators*, the logical framework has tended to encourage greater emphasis on quantitative measurement of inputs and outputs. However, efforts have also been made to apply it to process or social development projects. The most obvious way to do this is to identify proxy indicators for project

Table 8:   A logical framework matrix

Narrative summary	Objectively verifiable indicators (OVI)	Means of verification (MOV)	Important assumptions
Goal	Measures of goal achievement	Sources of information Methods used	Assumptions affecting purpose-goal linkage
Purpose	End of project status	Sources of information Methods used	Assumptions affecting inputs-outputs linkage
Outputs	Magnitudes of outputs Planned completion date	Sources of information Methods used	Assumptions affecting inputs-outputs linkage
Inputs	Nature and level of resources necessary Cost Planned starting date	Sources of information	Initial assumptions about the project

Source: Coleman (1987)

goals (number of community meetings held as a proxy for community organization etc. – see Harding, 1991, for example) but this may result in distortions in project implementation as described in Section 2.3. A more promising resolution, suggested by Riddell and Robinson (1992), is to accept that the best available form of 'objective verification' is the judgement of an independent evaluator on the extent of agreement about project impact among different groups affected by it. They also discuss different techniques of enquiry for eliciting the opinion of different groups, including focused discussions with members of particular categories of people (women, labourers, junior staff etc.).

A more fundamental problem of the logical framework is that although it does at least acknowledge the importance of external variables (assumptions) to project impact, it tends to enshrine the project blueprint and therefore reduces project flexibility and participation. Several NGOs have tried to circumvent this by establishing formal procedures for modification of the framework when projects are reviewed. With this flexibility built in, the framework itself can be used as a focus for participatory group discussions in a way that lengthy project proposal documents cannot. However, it may still be the case that the attempt to ensure unanimity of view between different project participants and staff may itself suppress local initiative.

Planning investments in infrastructure

The location of new facilities such as roads, clinics, schools and government offices is extremely important to rural areas, being a major determinant of access to different services and to the wider cash economy. In most countries, demand for new infrastructure is articulated through the mainstream of the political process, and far exceeds budgetary provisions. Rationing is then effected through an awkward combination of political favouritism and technical screening based on detailed quantitative information (census returns, maps etc.).

Box 12:   Where have all the farmers gone?

I was transferred to the Provincial Agricultural Marketing Department, in a hot and humid part of Latin America, at the time that a multi-million dollar grains marketing and storage project was about to be submitted for funding to an international donor. The project proposal had already been prepared, and represented several man-years of technical work, with detailed cost benefit analysis and initial specifications and capacity worked out for all the major investments.

However, a short visit (squeezed into a tight schedule for updating project costs!) to some of the main areas of production revealed that the number of farmers, on the basis of which marketed surplus and the need for buying centres had been calculated, had been grossly over-estimated. Further enquiry indicated that many farmers had moved north in search of better land, or were working as labourers in coca fields where wages were much higher. It was clear that many of the proposed buying centres would be white elephants.

Qualitative enquiry can play an important role in the latter by providing cross-checks against quantitative data. This is particularly important when, as is often the case, the original data on population, traffic flows and so on is out-of-date (see Box 12). Rapid appraisal can then serve to check whether the data is still accurate or not. It may also be useful to obtain information on some of the community level variables often neglected, as described in Section 3.4.

Qualitative enquiry has an even more significant role to play in the design phase of new infrastructure. First, elaborate mechanisms for consultation familiar in industrial countries are often absent. There is a need for alternative forms of enquiry to check that costs as well as

77

benefits of new infrastructure to local people are carefully weighed. Local knowledge also may be extremely useful, in choosing the precise location of buildings and bridges, selecting the best route for roads, warning about subsidence and flooding problems associated with particular sites, suggesting adaptations to basic building designs and so on.

Second, local participation in planning is absolutely necessary if the community is expected to bear some of the running costs of the new facilities – as is increasingly common, particularly in much of Africa. A willingness on the part of the local community to contribute to the capital costs of the project is also a guarantee of community commitment to a project – certainly more reliable than the word of local politicians, who may be more interested in obtaining kickbacks on the building contracts.

New infrastructure that involves forced relocation of farmers (government-sponsored villagization, construction of roads, imposition of large-scale irrigation, the flooding of reservoirs, establishment of farm settlement schemes) generates a large demand for ancillary planning information. Belshaw (1981b) provides a useful case study of the need to adjust methods of enquiry with the scale and pace of village relocation in Tanzania. It is particularly important to avoid divisions between those trained for physical planning (civil engineers) and those who must determine cropping systems and settlement requirements (Conyers, 1982; Cairncross et al., 1980).

Scudder (1982), generalizing from worldwide experience, observes that most relocated communities go through four distinct stages: initial trauma, shock, rehabilitation and stagnation. The first two stages are self-explanatory. The third arises when people have recovered sufficiently to take advantage of new economic opportunities (including previously uncultivated soil) and the special provisions arising from relocation begin to have force. Relocated communities enter into the fourth stage, stagnation, when these initial windfalls have been exhausted. Long-term qualitative feedback derived from surveys, village case studies and key informants can help to monitor the progress of communities through these stages and to identify ways of speeding up the first two and countering the fourth.

Public sector services
Planning expansion, reform or contraction of public services (in the fields of health, education or agricultural extension) requires as much detailed information as the planning of physical infrastructure. There are decisions to be made about which communities to serve and how, what kinds of transport and communications are needed, staffing requirements and where staff will live and work. While, in practice, these are usually dealt with informally within the agency concerned, larger changes (such as extending or cutting back on farmer support services for a new crop or

Table 9:   Some basic monitoring information needs for rural health, education and extension services

	Routinely-collected monitoring information	Supplementary data requirements
Health	Clinic attendance figures Demographic statistics (births, illness, deaths) Anthropometic measurements (e.g. under five weights) Contraceptive use	Clinic coverage (as percent of total population) Reasons for non-attendance at clinics Morale of community health workers Hygiene, sanitation, nutrition and other health practices Reasons for variation in age-weight statistics Reliability of demographic statistics Attitudes towards family planning
Education	Pupil enrolment Daily attendance Truency/drop-outs Examination results	Proportion of all children attending school Reasons for truency, and dropping out Teacher and pupil morale Staff-parent relations Reasons for variation in attendance and exam results
Agricultural extension	Crop area and yield estimates Farmers visited Demonstration plots organized Adoption rates (e.g. of new seeds)	Reliability of crop and yield statistics Morale of extension workers and relations with farmers Reasons for non-adoption

area) may justify more formal quantitative and qualitative enquiry to fill information gaps; including the agency and community-level variables described in Section 2.4.

Qualitative enquiry is also important in routine monitoring and evaluation of service department activities. The second column of Table 9 provides a rough checklist of statistical information often routinely collected in the fields of health, education and agricultural statistics. The third column then lists supplementary information required to interpret these statistics. Most can be collected using either quantitative or qualitative methods. Some are generally more suited to quantitative enquiry: e.g. estimating coverage of monthly health clinics (i.e. attendance as a percentage of the total population). Others are better suited to qualitative enquiry – gauging the morale of village level staff and their relationship with clients, for example. Usually, the choice of method of enquiry depends upon additional factors, including resources and time available.

Marketing
There can be few areas of activity in which governments and aid agencies have a record of such uninformed intervention as in the field of marketing, particularly agricultural marketing. Prices have been controlled, monopoly procurement decreed, property confiscated in defence of exploited consumers and producers alike – and all with very little detailed empirical enquiry into the efficiency of the marketing system affected. In fact, traditional marketing systems are often exceedingly sophisticated, performing storage, handling, transport and processing activities with an efficiency that the public sector has rarely proved able to match. This is not to deny that the public sector has an important role to play: in regulating competition, facilitating major new investments in infrastructure, establishing good marketing practices (including quality standards), and in providing market information. The point is that such activities require far more systematic enquiry into existing marketing systems than has been the norm.

Table 10 provides a list of minimal and more complete information about any particular marketing system that should be available prior to any public intervention. Estimates of overall flows of produce along different links in the marketing chain obviously require quantitative enquiry – though 'back of an envelope' calculations may be adequate for many purposes, and should be used to assess the reliability of formal estimates that may miss out significant illegal flows. Likewise qualitative enquiry may be useful in checking the reliability of official price data.

Data on quantities and prices alone, however, is virtually meaningless without a detailed understanding of contextual details that must be obtained direct from producers, consumers and traders through interviews. The sensitive nature of much of the information (profit margins, price-setting mechanisms, credit relations, smuggling etc.) means that qualitative enquiry – particularly that derived from key informants – is

Table 10:   Checklist of marketing information needs

Absolute minimum

○ A simple flow diagram identifying main types of traders, their marketing functions and the direction of flows between them. Some idea of which groups of traders are most powerful.

○ Some historical price data and information on seasonal variation in production and consumption.

○ An estimate of the overall volume and value of trade through the system, and of key technical parameters, e.g. the conversion ratio from paddy to rice.

Comprehensive

○ Estimates of the number and size-distribution of the main groups of traders, and the strength of group identity (trade organisations etc).

○ Estimates of the relative importance of flows along different channels.

○ Estimates of cost structures and profit margins of the main groups of traders.

○ Seasonal patterns of trade, prices and stocks.

○ Historical data on production, consumption, imports, exports and factors likely to influence them.

○ Details of past interventions and their impact.

likely to be more productive than formal surveys (see Chapters by Harriss and Christensen in Devereux and Hoddinott, 1993). Traders often have much to hide, and a legacy of uninformed and often hostile intervention has left them deeply wary of officials who ask questions. This makes rural enquiry into marketing particularly difficult – but also extremely satisfying if successful!

After a year and a half of interviewing agricultural traders in Bolivia (and before ever hearing of the existence of RRA) one of the authors wrote out the following list of tips on interviewing traders:

1. write down and memorize beforehand exactly what you want to find out, and check through the list at the end of the interview;
2. state clearly and confidently your purpose and why you require the information, and always carry credentials or an introductory letter;
3. never hurry, and be prepared to listen to irrelevant chat, if it helps the interviewee to relax;
4. try to avoid peak trading times, and if the interviewee is busy then arrange another time to visit;
5. leave the most sensitive questions until the end;

6. find out and use the same units of measure as traders themselves, and adapt questions about frequency and quantity of purchases to the practices of traders themselves;
7. always obtain data about the terms of transactions (including credit arrangements) with both buyers and sellers.

Box 13:   The much-maligned coffee roasters of Bolivia

Amid much interest in promoting coffee production in Bolivia, we were asked to undertake a study of the domestic market. Official statistics on consumption published by the Coffee Board, and Ministry of Trade diverged so wildly that we decided to cross check them against a rapid survey of roasters in one or two of the major cities. Attempts to locate the mostly quite small roasting companies proved extremely difficult, however; initial efforts ran into steel gates, large dogs and stony faces. Through informal contacts, however, we were able to meet up with the young manager of one of the larger family businesses.

The reason for their suspicions quickly became apparent. At the wholesale level, the roasters found themselves competing with coffee exporters (generally a much more lucrative business), while at the retail level they were squeezed by often unrealistic government price controls. The result was that coffee supply rarely met demand; and it was the roasters who were often blamed, rather than the government that engineered the shortages by imposing unrealistic margins on the trade. Shortages encouraged adulteration of the coffee – for which roasters were again blamed. Once we had reassured our key informant that our interest was in overall market prospects, rather than roasting margins, it took only a few telephone calls to obtain the information we required.

The research also cast light on widespread rumours that coffee was heavily adulterated – ox-blood being one of the most gleefully-cited ingredients. The squeeze on margins had indeed resulted in adulteration – with caramelized sugar – but consumers had become so accustomed to the resulting flavour that they would not drink it any other way!

Source: Copestake et al. (1986)

Savings and credit programmes
Commercially-successful banking operations, even in rural areas, are generally based on tried and tested quantitative methods for both appraisal of borrowers and monitoring of branch performance.

○ Borrower appraisal. It is useful for bank staff to be able to make an accurate appraisal of the trustworthiness of potential borrowers, but such judgements are generally backed up by formal references, guarantees and collateral requirements; and larger loans will only be sanctioned after detailed technical and financial analysis of proposed investments.

○ Branch performance. Assessment of the performance of individual branches and their staff, on the other hand, is largely based on analysis of financial statistics – deposit mobilization, increased lending and repayment ratios. Line managers generally trust their own experience and judgement, rather than quantitative analysis, when it comes to explaining why performance has been better or worse than expected and whether anybody should be rewarded or penalized accordingly.

The situation is very different, however, in publicly-owned or regulated financial institutions that are mandated to meet economic and social, as well as financial goals. Economic goals may entail meeting targets for disbursement of loans to specified sectors, and providing credit at subsidized interest rates: while social goals may entail providing finance to disadvantaged social groups, such as small-scale farmers, and improving access to credit by reducing collateral requirements.

Such policies generally involve trade offs between profitability, economic growth and equity and mean that performance cannot be assessed exclusively on the basis of financial data (Copestake, 1988). They also force junior bank staff to approve large numbers of small loans without binding guarantees and on the basis of extremely rapid assessments of the potential borrowers and their plans.

Qualitative enquiry is certainly relevant here. Imagine the situation faced by a manager freshly appointed to a bank branch in an Indian village. His (there are still few women rural branch managers in India) first and most dreaded task is to review overall branch performance indicators, particularly the structure of overdue or problem loan accounts. If these make up a large part of the loan portfolio, then he will have to spend much time and effort on debt collection, and the scope for new lending may be limited. Having run through the loan ledgers, taking particular note of who his most important depositors and borrowers are (good relations with these people will be vital) the manager's next task is to review the micro-economy of the area. Who are the richest and most influential people? Who are the poorest? What activities are profitable and expanding? Virtually the whole repertoire of qualitative enquiry methodology may be needed to answer these questions.

Where banks have a clear poverty focus, they have indeed begun to institutionalize some of the qualitative techniques we have been discussing. Appraisal and loan supervizion through small borrower groups is perhaps the leading example. More recently, government and bank staff have also begun to use participatory methods such as wealth ranking and 'pass the stick' to identify the poorest households for receipt of subsidized loans (Chandramouli, 1990).

Disaster response

There is an urgent need to compare the effectiveness of different qualitative and quantitative methods in forecasting and responding to drought and famine. The 1983-85 African drought provided almost a laboratory setting for the comparative analysis of national decisionmaking, donor responses and the types of information various NGOs employed in first raising the alarm. While donors have tended to view disaster response as a macro-issue to be revealed by national food balance studies, disasters originate and are experienced by specific communities and individuals. Thus in many countries, acute distress has been experienced at the 'micro' local without appropriate action being taken at the 'macro' level to provide relief and anticipate future needs (see Box 4).

A principal reason disaster planning has in the past been so poor is the fact that it depends upon a good linkage between these levels. National food balance studies alone, based on often patchy and unreliable census data, are clearly not adequate (see section 3.2).

Anderson International Associates (1987) argue that in considering how such linkages can be strengthened we should distinguish early warning systems (EWS) from disaster response mechanisms. Both can be problematic, and both can be improved through adapted qualitative enquiry, with initial (often qualitative) reports triggering a rapid accumulation of more detailed information. Frankenberger (1991) identifies the Rapid Food Security Assessment as a key step in such an escalation of response; Table 11 is an adaptation of his list of the information such assessments can usefully provide.

This brief discussion of disaster response leads into the more general need for monitoring of natural resources. We are increasingly aware that for poorer farmers, the collapse of the commons and the destruction of trees and woodland can remove traditional options for coping with disaster. It becomes important to estimate rates of resource depletion and degrees of environmental stress. Obviously, where good quantitative measurement is feasible it should be used. But in many areas planners must instead rely upon very crude indicators of environmental stress, and this has become a focus of RRA.

Sensitive topics

Another domain where qualitative enquiry may be the only feasible approach is in regard to highly sensitive issues: politically-charged topics,

84

Table 11:   Data requirements for rapid food security assessment

A   *Leading indicators*
1. Evidence of, and reasons for, crop failure (rainfall, poor access to seeds and other inputs, pest damage etc.).
2. Evidence of deterioration in rangelands conditions (unusual migration patterns, animal deaths, young female animals being offered for sale, increased concentrations of cattle at slaughtering places and in the kraals of wealthy households).
3. Market conditions (food price increases, unseasonal shortages, unemployment among labourers and artisans, low level of household food stocks).

B   *Concurrent indicators*
Unexpected migration, sale of capital goods (jewellery, implements, draught animals, land), increased demand for credit, increased dependence upon wild foods, reduction in number of meals, increased reliance on inter-household exchange.

C   *Trailing indicators*
Malnutrition, morbidity, mortality, land degradation, land sales, consumption of seed, permanent migration.

D   *Supplementary information – needed for planning relief*
Food use and food preferences, condition of livestock, fodder availability, market access and cash reserves, availability of wild foods, special food requirements for child-bearing women and for weaning infants, prevalent health problems, available transport and storage facilities, other organizations in the area involved or who could be involved in relief (including local NGOs) and possible mechanisms for co-ordination.

E   *Supplementary information – in areas of conflict*
Conflict zones, level and type of violence, implications for access, relations between forces and other organizations in the area.

Source: Frankenberger (1991)

illegal behaviours, or matters of extreme controversy. For example, donors might want to know how corrupt the local administration has become. Are bribes being paid routinely? Can individuals buy better assignments? Are project staff siphoning off resources meant for beneficiaries? (see Box 14) These are all legitimate questions, with major implications for the planning and management of field projects. And yet they are very difficult to address effectively by means of the usual quantitative survey. The answers people give, when pressed, will be 'for the record', and may not reflect their true opinions. An experienced investigator working discreetly behind the scene with a few key informants may produce a more reliable, albeit qualitative, estimate of the actual situation. (Indeed, the compilation of political intelligence, whether by governments or by rivals, requires precisely this kind of approach.)

Box 14:   The smell of corruption?

We are a team of three, arriving to examine in the field several small projects designed to reprovision people after a major famine and supported by a sponsoring NGO. Two of us are field managers from elsewhere in the continent and one an NGO field official from a third country.

We are told one project cannot be examined in any depth, because the project files were stolen from an open vehicle while it was parked in the market. Since this happened just before the local manager was to have been audited we wonder: Why did the thieves steal nothing else?

At the second project, now also under local control and nearing its termination, nothing goes as planned. On arrival, the local manager appears slightly drunk and the vehicle promised by headquarters is nowhere to be seen. Nor have any plans been made for the necessary field visits. After prodding, the local manager takes us the next day to see a trader, who is in turn very accommodating, even effusive. We all notice, independently, and discuss this among ourselves. The next morning, arriving early at the project office – some twenty miles from the trader's store – we encounter him leaving. He scurries away without greeting or explanation. And again we wonder. Then, near the end of our four-day visit, we meet a volunteer after hours who tells us the local staff member has gone into trading for himself, using the remaining project resources for his start. Nothing conclusive, obviously, but enough to cause all three of us to decide something is amiss.

However, when I convey these sentiments to the NGO headquarters in the distant capital city, the NGO representative gets quite angry. No, emphatically. As far as they can see, there is no corruption in their projects. They think outsiders have no business carrying unfounded rumours back to headquarters.

Turbulent conditions

Finally, there are occasions when important policy decisions must be taken, but either the time is short or field conditions are so turbulent that no in depth field investigation is possible. In 1988, for example, reports surfaced from Southern Sudan that human slavery had re-emerged among starving Nuer ex-nomads seeking to escape the intolerable conditions they were encountering in their home communities. On the one hand, such reports, if true, would indicate the extreme stresses faced by Nuer refugees. On the other hand, these same conditions made it extremely difficult for concerned NGOs to verify the scope of the problems at source. Were these simply isolated occurrences, or was this an emergent trend affecting many refugees? Obviously, we cannot expect a qualitative enquiry on such an issue to provide a conclusive answer. Nevertheless, a carefully-conducted qualitative examination of the problem ought to provide a better basis for action than simply repeating garbled anecdotal accounts. In the 1990s we are seeing the return of conditions like those recorded for medieval Europe: famines, plagues, ethnic cleansing, 1000 per cent annual inflation, warlordism, and mass population movements out of combat zones. Those seeking to extend help under such conditions may have no choice but to employ qualitative methods when trying to assess more accurately the problems they face.

4.3 Opportunities and constraints

We have argued throughout this book that opportunities for practitioners to improve their use of qualitative enquiry are numerous. If so, then it is necessary to consider why these opportunities have not been taken up.

It is worth reiterating that qualitative *sources* are being used all the time, but in an unsystematic and often officially unrecognized way. In our own work, we have repeatedly observed that an individual will buttress his or her arguments with personal anecdotes derived from friends, from visits home, from recent field tours, or from field experience perhaps many years earlier. Often such references are being used to illustrate general principles that may indeed be sound and relevant to the current problem. But to base decisions entirely on such anecdotal material without any systematic cross-checking is at best unprofessional and at worst highly dangerous and irresponsible. It has also prejudiced those with a more rigorous training against all use of qualitative sources, encouraging a retreat to the opposite extreme of expensive over-reliance upon quantitative approaches.

In the remainder of this chapter we look briefly at some of the constraints to improved use of qualitative enquiry under three broad headings:

1. outstanding weaknesses in methodology;

2. individual ignorance and scepticism;
3. institutional constraints.

In each case we also consider the scope for overcoming these constraints.

Methodological weaknesses and research

The systematic application of qualitative enquiry to specific policy problems is relatively recent in many fields; experience in what works and what doesn't work is still being accumulated. Disciplinary specialization has also constrained exchanges of experiences, cross-fertilization of ideas, and identification of best practice.

More research and documentation of the use of qualitative enquiry, in language *accessible to non-specialists*, can help to overcome these constraints, and to fill in gaps. For example, we have seen that most rural areas are now crowded with different government and non-government agencies, and that many rural development activities depend heavily for their success upon the presumed performance of other agencies under separate control. There is a major need for improving the methodology for rapid assessment of different agencies, and identification of gaps, duplication and interaction between them.

More systematic empirical research into the cost-effectiveness and reliability of different methods of enquiry (quantitative and qualitative), such as that by Franzel and Crawford (1987), is also needed. Such research should help to clarify how qualitative enquiry establishes the validity, applicability and limits of its information – see Box 13. It is instructive here to compare information obtained from key informants in the field and the handling of rival 'expert' technical opinions obtained by consultants. Such sources have at least two things in common: both depend for acceptance upon one's regard for the source, and both are judged primarily by the face validity of the information. Distrust over qualitative sources often arises from the concern that such information is inherently biased and anecdotal. To counter this fear (widely shared among quantitative analysts), proponents of qualitative enquiry must clarify how they exercise data quality control (an old topic in anthropology, see Naroll (1962), though not yet adequately addressed in the RRA literature).

Another area where further methodological refinement is needed is in the closer integration of qualitative and quantitative studies. We have seen how qualitative information can greatly improve the application of certain quantitative techniques, through field checking of assumptions, better framing of questionnaires and more astute choice of study sites. Often, too, those carrying out conventional quantitative research accumulate a large stock of qualitative information which might change how the results are viewed if analysts took the time to listen. There is a particularly strong case for employing qualitative enquiry prior to stratification of a population, which researchers often carry out in an intuitive and informal way, or on the basis of *a priori* analysis.

Box 15: Participatory wealth ranking in Zambia

As part of its response to the 1992 drought, the Government of Zambia asked NGOs in each district to identify 'the poorest of the poor' eligible for free relief in each of the communities where they worked. On hearing this, I decided to try to encourage a local NGO to undertake a wealth-ranking exercise following the method developed by Grandin (1981). The project had previously avoided targeting its work, in deference to the highly egalitarian culture; and despite the existence of clear inequalities of wealth and income.

On meeting the Community Development Coordinator I discovered that he had already developed his own qualitative methodology for identifying the poorest of the poor. In each community he was organizing a meeting of:

1. the headman – 'because he knows peoples' names and how much land they cultivate'
2. religious leaders – 'because they understand who the poor are from the Bible'
3. the co-op manager – 'because he sees how much money people spend in the shop'.

If these three groups can agree, he says, then he could have a reliable list.

Grandin (1991) argues that it is more accurate to obtain wealth rankings from each key informant separately, and then work out an average ranking arithmetically. But the co-ordinator disagreed – expressing a strong preference for consensus over arithmetic.

Ignorance and training

Lack of awareness among practitioners of the enormous body of literature on qualitative enquiry is quite staggering. Even those with social science degrees (particularly economists) are often unaware of the diversity and pedigree of relevant literature in other branches of social science, geography and history – an ignorance which enables them to maintain a blanket scepticism towards all forms of qualitative enquiry.

Persuading often overloaded senior staff (see next section) to take time out either for study, or to conduct field work themselves is never easy – even with a promise of improved efficiency in the long run as a pay-off.

However, qualitative enquiry may actually make smaller, rather than greater demands on senior staff time when compared to the planning, supervision, analysis and interpretation of quantitative surveys, whose reliability is often undermined anyway by the poor quality of data collected by inadequately trained, supervized and motivated field staff.

The scope for increased formal training in qualitative enquiry is therefore large: both within university curricula, and more importantly through professional courses, in-house training and networking. Such training should cover not only the basic techniques and steps (planning, interviewing, validation, analysis, presentation etc.), but also the use of multiple methods, the importance of validation through triangulation, and the difficult trade-offs between coverage, detail, relevance, cost and timeliness.

This work has already begun, initially under the label of FSR, but more recently and importantly through the expansion of RRA and RPA expertize and networks. Much of it is taking place through direct interaction between practitioners without regard to disciplinary lines, though its impact has to date been far greater within NGOs than government agencies. We suggest that the latter are only likely to respond through increased academic interest in qualitative enquiry and its inclusion in both natural and social science postgraduate curricula.

Bureaucracy and institutional reform

It would be a mistake, however, to attribute the limited use of qualitative enquiry to lack of academic respectability, and individual ignorance or scepticism. We have both frequently encountered individual managers and administrators (generally within large and hierarchical organizations) who are either unfamiliar with or conditioned against *any* form of problem-solving enquiry – whether qualitative or quantitative. Such mental blockages can generally be attributed as much to institutional and cultural context as to individual ignorance or scepticism, and can probably be overcome by training only in conjunction with more general institutional reform.

We can elaborate upon this observation by presenting a brief caricature of the civil service tradition inherited and adapted during the colonial period, which continues to employ a large proportion of salaried staff in many countries. In such organizations, senior administrators are typically regarded as being responsible for all their subordinates' actions, and thereby encouraged to take unto themselves almost all the organization's planning, co-ordinating, delegating and reporting functions. At the same time, they impose strict rules on what their subordinates (including technical and professional staff in non-line positions) are allowed to do.

Those of us who have worked in such systems are familiar with the rules: all letters to be signed by the Department Head, no direct lateral communication except on the most minor matters permitted, all cheques to be signed by the Head, all travel authorizations to go to the Head and so forth. This can be termed the *hub-and-wheel* style of management, where the person in authority deals directly with a circle of subordinates to ensure that organizational tasks are carried out. It suited colonial situations, where senior administrators were expected to work through junior staff who were either relatively untrained, or untrusted. But, because those attaining senior positions have a vested interest in preserving a system that gave them such power, it has proved extremely durable.

An important feature of this form of administration is the rigid separation of policy from implementation. While policy is under review, subordinates are not supposed to comment publicly and any upwards pressure or information may be unwelcome. But once policy changes have been determined, subordinates are still not supposed to comment either, despite the fact that their presence in the field often enables them to give relevant advice. Expatriate advisors play an important role in the system – welcomed because they can give advice to senior staff without the latter risking losing face by being seen to consult subordinates.

When officials are younger and hold responsible positions at field level, they are too busy doing what they are told to undertake any extended qualitative enquiry. Later, when they do reach policymaking positions at the Provincial or National levels, the combination of workload and behavioural expectations again make it difficult. Thus structures and attitudinal tendencies combine to frustrate decisionmaking based on upward flow of current and reasonably accurate qualitative information. Outsiders, on the other hand, can be asked to conduct qualitative enquiry 'cold' (i.e. without prior knowledge of an area or problem) and be reasonably sure of a hearing upon their return.

However, perhaps the most serious limitation of rural bureaucracies is their limited ability to accommodate multiple or modulated interventions, tailored to the conditions and needs of different areas. One of the most important justifications of formal enquiry, whether quantitative or qualitative, is to enable agencies to be more responsive in this way. The inability to cope with diversity can be attributed in part to external pressure for horizontal equity i.e. equal treatment for all. But the more important explanation is that diversity is difficult for highly-centralized policymaking units to handle. The result, only too often, is recourse to standard guidelines and arbitrary rules: one farmer training centre per zone, one hospital per district and so on. Rural enquiry that challenges the assumptions underlying such uniformity is unlikely to be well received.

It would, however, be misleading to end this section on a negative note. Increased and better use of qualitative enquiry can improve the efficiency and responsiveness even of highly bureaucratic organizations, by keeping senior staff more in touch with reality in the field. Moreover, while cuts in public expenditure associated with structural adjustment programmes are having severe social and economic effects, they can also create genuine opportunities to overcome some of these bureaucratic constraints.

Box 16:   A little test

Information once written down in print tends to acquire a degree of authenticity that may be completely unwarranted.

All but one of the instances described in the twelve boxes in this paper are based on actual experiences of one or other of us, subject to our own interpretation and memory limitations. However one of the boxes, although plausible, is entirely fictitious. Can you determine – from internal evidence alone – which one it is?

The point of this exercise is that it is often impossible to assess reliability of information on the basis of internal consistency alone – hence the importance of using more than one source and method of enquiry.

---

5 The Future of Qualitative Enquiry

OUR REVIEW of qualitative enquiry has emphasized the special advantages of such methods for rural development and policy-related decisions. Nevertheless, analysts who are choosing how to investigate real world problems and issues do not do so on the basis of abstract considerations of cost-effectiveness, suitability, and validity. Rather, they respond to proximate trends and their own perceptions of what is expected of them. In this concluding chapter we consequently examine the larger context which influences which modes of enquiry decisionmakers adopt, in order to anticipate future uses of qualitative enquiry.

5.1 Contemporary trends

Perhaps the most significant influence upon all types of enquiry is the vastly increasing power of personal computers, whose awesome number handling capabilities push users toward preplanned, quantitative forms of analysis. A recent work entitled *Rural Information Systems* (Buse and Driscoll, 1992) is entirely given over to examination of data transfers and the integration of results from large data bases, all fundamentally quantitative in nature. Just as in the 1970s project planning became the universal format applied to all types of rural development activity, so in the 1980s policy analysis became equally pervasive (Section 3.1). Since this means in practice employing micro-economic methods for weighing policy options, we can predict strong pressure towards increasingly quantitative analysis even for macro-economic issues which seem unsuitable for such applications (House and Shull, 1991). The widespread adoption of project appraisal at the micro-level and policy analysis matrices at the macro-level leaves little apparent scope for qualitative enquiry, mainly because these are demanding applications which pre-empt the time and resources which otherwise might have been devoted to more general concerns. As House and Shull warn (1991:1), '*Some* numbers beat *no* numbers every time'.

Added pressure toward quantified analyses comes from the spread of geographic information systems (GIS) and management information systems (MIS) into the domain of development planning. Of course, both types of software have been available for some time in the respective fields of geography and management. Now, however, GIS and MIS are coming into widespread use in rural development. Both seem to offer the prospect of integrating all forms of subsidiary data handling, GIS for spatially-related data and MIS for longitudinal, program/project-related data. To have almost instantaneous access at one's fingertips to such an array of data sources is an awesome power. No matter that in practice there are still many problems associated with these technologies; their promise is sufficient that we predict they will absorb large amounts of resources in the near and medium future.

Meanwhile (as we warn in Section 4.2) nearly all data gathering for purposes of facilitating rural development is conceptualized by donors within the format of the project cycle. This lends legitimacy to many different types of field enquiry: questions about household activities, the role of women, who gets what, energy implications, 'downstream' impacts, and so forth. The cost is the increased formalism and the tight, sequential structuring of data-gathering activities. There is a strong, implicit assumption that somehow by increasing the fineness of detail, the scope of data coverage, and the comprehensiveness of models we can avoid making unsupported judgements in any vital area of the project/programme domain. Wisdom is seen to reside in an 'expert system' rather than in real people. Obviously, we do not share this expectation, at least not in its more extreme forms, where project planning becomes a substitute for the judicious exercise of field intelligence.

It is not sufficient to decry these trends. They would not be happening if they were not answering, to some degree, real world information requirements. The modern organization with its internal 'technostructure' of information-related specialties (accountants, controllers, planners, media specialists, and the like) has an immense appetite for processed information. Those working within increasingly bureaucratized service agencies have little choice but to supply the types of information the system demands. (This is even becoming true of organizational functioning in NGOs and private foundations.)

Instead, we have pointed out in these pages that there are vigorous countervailing trends, sometimes led by the very people who initially sponsored highly quantified work (eg Patton in educational evaluation). We see an emerging consensus behind much of the thinking in the three fields of qualitative evaluation, action research, and collaborative research. An urgent task for development practitioners is to review this body of field-tested, qualitative enquiry in order to identify common lessons which may also apply in the sphere of rural development. We hope this small book makes a usable beginning in this direction, but recognize there is much additional synthesis which ought to be feasible given the wealth of sources on our topic within different professional specialties.

5.2 Future directions

There are, then, several directions rural development enquiry is likely to take in the near and medium future. We anticipate four major developments, all growing out of tendencies already visible within development activities.

Real-time surveys
Computer technologies have reached a stage where rural development enquiry can achieve an almost immediate 'turn-around': the results being returned to clients while investigators are still in the field. There is no reason not to exploit this advantage. As more investigators demonstrate 'real time' capability we expect such performance gradually will become the norm. An immediate advantage is that conclusions can be field checked with respondents within days (or a week or two at most), providing a major opportunity for eliminating erroneous interpretations and increasing respondents' sense of 'ownership' of their distilled experiences. Furthermore, the ability to generate graphs, tables, and a glossy publication at the site should greatly facilitate the distribution of reports to all interested 'stakeholders'. Many of users' complaints about out-dated results, incomplete analysis or irrelevant recommendations should diminish once rapid turn-around becomes normal practice.

At the same time, we warn that this capability for on-site analysis and interpretation puts even greater pressure upon the qualitative dimensions of an enquiry. In these pages we have argued that good quantitative enquiry presumes an accompanying qualitative effort to field-check questions, to correctly locate samples, and to interpret results meaningfully. The extended timetable allowed to past surveys left room to correct errors and check interpretations (though admittedly many studies failed to use such opportunities). Now, however, exploratory discussions, sampling, field questioning, data analysis, and report writing must all occur in a single, intensive burst of activity. It becomes even more important for field investigators to recognize the places where survey designs presume an accompanying qualitative understanding of the system being studied. Giving 'real-time' results to clients means getting it right in the very first instance – an exceedingly demanding expectation when the topics are only imperfectly understood by those gathering data.

Specialized PRA/RRA
The same pressures towards procedural elaboration which have driven the growth of formal methodologies for data analysis also impinge upon new

forms of qualitative enquiry. In particular, we see domain-specific applications of participatory rural appraisal (or RRA as it is still termed in the USA) emerging, oriented toward the distinctive needs of emergency relief, policy assessment, social forestry, and other potential uses. Having field-tested checklists at hand in a given area of enquiry can be a major advantage when time is short and the investigators somewhat unfamiliar with their topic (see Gow's review of RRA in Finsterbusch, Ingersoll and Llewellyn, 1990).

The approach adopted by Conway, McCracken and Pretty (1988) at IIED in London emphasized RRA as a 'toolkit' from which users would select the most relevant methods, while also identifying four main classes: (1) exploratory, (2) topical, (3) participatory, and (4) monitoring RRA. The literature is already moving rapidly beyond treating the array of existing methods as a simple menu from which field workers make selections as needed. In so doing, cross-linkages to other literatures should become more apparent. This has already been discussed with respect to farming systems research, but also applies to other literatures, including: policy 'mapping' (Chapter 5 in White, 1990); opportunity analysis (Keller in Sampath and Young, 1990); and 'resource profiling' in the analysis of poverty (e.g. Lewis, 1993).

Disaster response
Fifteen years ago few of us would have guessed that disaster relief in one form or another would have become a major preoccupation of donors in the 1990s. Between AIDS, civil war, volcanic eruptions, ethnic cleansing, prolonged droughts, home-grown terrorism, banditry, and now nuclear proliferation, Third World policymakers face awesome challenges. Refugee populations number in the millions, and continue to grow with each new conflict. Entire countries have lapsed back into warlord governance. Circumstances and needs change with astonishing speed, and the ways in which relief may exacerbate or prolong conflict are increasingly well understood (see for example, Duffield, 1993). Such circumstances put a premium upon having access to broadly correct, timely information, in situations where qualitative enquiry may be the only feasible option other than pure guesswork. Thus we make no apology for our stress upon the potential advantages of such methods; in broad areas of the world major decisions must be taken which can draw only upon qualitative assessments. We suggest donors should encourage those with field experience in RRA and PRA to share their knowledge of the performance of various field instruments under real world, crisis conditions.

Bureaucratization of NGO/PVO activities

Reluctantly, we observe also the growth of middle management within voluntary agencies and private foundations. It is ironic that at a time when donors are more willing to fund initiatives undertaken by NGOs, the recipient organizations are themselves becoming more like the top-heavy governmental and corporate institutions they are replacing. In earlier sections of this book we warned that the typical, small NGO can least afford unnecessary formalism (such as 'improved' M&E and MIS procedures). With sharply-constrained limits to overhead costs, the small NGO must remain action-oriented and flexible. We have tried to show that whereas qualitative enquiry is not a universal answer to all data-handling needs, it does possess intrinsic strengths which can be exploited by managers who must work within tight budgets and relatively short time horizons. Of all the various types of corporate institutions which may employ systematic enquiry, NGOs have the highest incentive to take the methods and perspective we have reviewed seriously.

5.3 Conclusion

We conclude, then, on a note of some urgency. The on-going transformation of rural development management into preplanned and rigid routines dictated by distant financiers is a fact. The reformulation of many data-oriented tasks to fit existing computer software is also a fact. The awesome data storage and retrieval capacities now available at remote field stations are a significant and underexploited potential, one which when properly pursued can remain low cost and flexible. However, this balance will not be achieved automatically. Unless users begin to exploit the equally great advantages of flexible, need-oriented qualitative enquiry, organizations will devote most of their resources towards more rigid, preplanned forms of mainly quantitative analysis. We have argued the case for employing both qualitative and quantitative approaches. Each type does certain tasks well. What we have tried to show is that qualitative modes of enquiry represent a particularly cost-effective answer to the kinds of information demand which rural development field agencies are likely to experience, both now and in the future.

References

Anderson International Associates (1987) *A Report on the problems and approaches to improved management of drought-famine*, Africa Bureau, USAID, Washington, DC.

Argyris, C., Putnam, R. and Smith, D. (1987) *Action Science*, Jossey-Bass, San Francisco, CA.

Arnon, I. (1975) 'Evaluation Methods', *The Planning and Programming of Agricultural Research*, FAO, Rome.

Arnon, I. (1989) *Agricultural Research and Technology Transfer*, Elsevier, London and New York.

Ascher, W. (1978) *Forecasting: An appraisal for policy-makers and planners*, Baltimore: Johns Hopkins.

Baker, D. (1992) 'The inability of farming systems research to deal with agricultural policy', Agricultural Research and Extension *Network Paper No.35*. ODI, London.

Barlett, P. (ed.) (1980) *Agricultural Decision-making: Anthropological contributions to rural development*, Academic Press, New York.

Behnke, R. (1985) 'Measuring the benefits of subsistence versus commercial livestock production in Africa', *Agricultural Systems*, Vol.16, pp.109–35.

Behnke, R. (1987) 'Cattle accumulation and the commercialisation of the traditional livestock industry in Botswana', *Agricultural Systems*, Vol.24, pp.1–29.

Belshaw, D.G.R. (1981) 'A theoretical framework for data-economising appraisal procedures with applications to rural development planning', *IDS Bulletin*, Vol.12, No.4, pp.12–22.

Belshaw, D.G.R. (1981) 'Village viability assessment procedures in Tanzania: Decision-making with curtailed information requirements', *Public Administration and Development*, Vol.1, pp.3–13.

Belshaw, D.G.R. and Hall, M. (1972) 'The analysis and use of agricultural experimental data in Tropical Africa', *East African Journal of Rural Development*, 5(1&2), pp.39-72.

Berdegué, J.A. (1992) 'Challenges to farming systems research and extension.' Agricultural Research and Extension *Network Paper No.34*. London: ODI.

Biggs, S.D. (1983) 'Informal and formal data collection methods in agricultural research programmes', Notes prepared for the Conference on Statistical policy in developing countries, IDS, Sussex, July 1983.

Biggs, S.D. (1991) 'Farming systems research and rural poverty; a political economy perspective on institutionalisation', Unpublished paper, prepared for FAO.

Bogdan, R. and Taylor, S. (1975) *Introduction to Qualitative Research Methods*, John Wiley, New York.

Booth, D. (1992) *New Directions in Social Development Research*, Cambridge University Press, Cambridge.

BRAC (1980) *The Net: Power structure in ten villages*, Bangladesh Rural Advancement Committee: 66 Mohathali Commercial Area, Dacca 12, Bangladesh.

Branch, K., Hooper, D.W., Thompson, J. and Creighton, J. (1984) *Guide to Social Assessment: A framework for assessing social change*, Westview Press, Boulder, CO.

Brandt, R.M. (1972) *Studying Behavior in Natural Settings*, Holt, Rinehart and Winston, New York.

Braun, G. (1991) 'Anti-Projects: Developing out of a dead-end', *Vierteljares berichte* No.125, pp.311–20.

Brewer, R.J. and Hunter, A. (1989) *Multi-method Research: A synthesis of styles*, Sage, Newbury Park, CA.

Brown, D. (1991) 'Methodological consideration in the evaluation of social development programmes: an alternative approach', *Community Development Journal*, Vol.26, No.4 pp.259–65.

Bunch, R. (1985) *Two Ears of Corn: A guide to people-centred agricultural improvement*, World Neighbors, Oklahoma City, OK.

Bunting, A.H. (ed.) (1987) *Agricultural Environments: Characterisation, classification, and mapping*, CAB International, Wallingford.

Burgess, R.G. (1984) *In the Field: An introduction to field research*, Allen and Unwin, London.

Burgess, R.G. (ed.) (1985) *Strategies for Educational Research: Qualitative methods*, Social research and educational studies series, No.1, The Falmer Press, Lewes and Philadelphia.

Buse, R.C. and Driscoll, J.L. (eds) (1992) *Rural Information Systems*, Iowa State University Press, Ames, IA.

Cairncross, S., Carruthers, I., Curtis, D., Feecham, R., Bradley, D. and Baldwin, G. (1980) *Evaluation for Village Water Supply Planning*, John Wiley, Chichester.

Campbell, D. (1979) 'Degrees of Freedom' and the Case Study, In T. Cook and C. Reichardt (eds), *Qualitative and Quantitative Methods in Evaluation Research*, Sage, Beverley Hills, CA.

Carruthers, I. and Chambers, R. (1981) 'Rapid appraisal for rural development', *Agricultural Administration*, Vol.10, pp.407–22.

Casley, D.J. and Kumar, K. (1987) *Project Monitoring and Evaluation in Agriculture*, John Hopkins Press, Baltimore, MD.

Casley, D.J. and Kumar, K. (1988) *The collection, analysis, and use of monitoring and evaluation data*, John Hopkins Press, Baltimore, MD.

Casley, D.J. and Lury, D.A. (1987) *Data Collection in Developing Countries*, Clarendon Press, Oxford.

Caws, P. (1989) 'The law of quality and quantity, or what numbers can and can't describe', In B. Glassner and J.D. Moreno (eds) (1989) *The Qualitative-quantitative Distinction in the Social Sciences*, Kluwer, London.

Cernea, M.M. (1990a) *From Unused Social Knowledge to Policy Creation: The case of population resettlement*, Harvard Institute for International Development, DP 342.

Cernea, M.M. (1990b) *Social Science Knowledge for Development Interventions*, Harvard Institute for International Development, DP 334.

Cernea, M.M. (1990c) *Re-tooling in applied social investigation for development planning: Some methodological issues*, Address to the International conference on rapid assessment methodologies for planning and evaluation of health related programs. Pan American Health Organisation, Washington DC, Nov. 12.

Cernea, M.M. (1991a) 'The socio-cultural dimension to development: The contribution of sociologists and social anthropologists to the work of development agencies', Workshop convened by GTZ, World Bank, Reprint Series: No.463

Cernea, M.M. (ed) (1991b) *Putting People First: Sociological variables in rural development*, New York: Oxford University Press for the World Bank.

Cernea, M.M., Coulter, J.K. and Russell, J.F.A. (eds) (1985) *Research-extension-farmer: A two-way continuum for agricultural development*, The World Bank, Washington DC.

Cernea, M.M. and Tepping, B. (1977) *A System for Monitoring and Evaluating Agricultural Extension Projects*, The World Bank, Washington, DC.

Chambers, R. (1980) *Rural Poverty Unperceived: Problems and remedies*, The World Bank, Washington, DC.

Chambers, R. (1983a) *Rapid Appraisal for Improving Existing Canal Irrigation Systems*, Ford Foundation, Delhi.

Chambers, R. (1983b) *Rural Development: Putting the last first*, Longman, London.

Chambers, R. (1991) 'Shortcut and participatory methods for gaining social information for projects.' In M.M. Cernea (ed.) (1991) *Putting People First: Sociological variables in rural development*, Oxford University Press for the World Bank, New York.

Chambers, R. and Jiggins, J. (1987) 'Agricultural research for resource-poor farmers. Part 1: transfer or technology and farming systems research', *Agricultural Administration and Extension* 27(1), pp.35–52.

Chambers, R. and Moris, J. (eds) (1973) *Mwea: An Irrigated Rice Settlement in Kenya*, Weltforum Verlag, Munich.

Chambers, R., Pacey, A. and Thrupp, L.A. (1989) *Farmer First: Farmer innovation and agricultural research*, IT Publications, London.

Chandramouli, K. (1991) '"Pass on the pen" approach: identifying the poorest of poor families', *RRA Notes* No.14, pp.29–32, IIED, London.

Clayton, E. (1983) 'Project management, monitoring and evaluation', In *Agriculture, Poverty and Freedom in Developing Countries*, Macmillan: London.

Cohen, R. (1973) *Warring Epistemologies: Quality and quantity in African research*, Northwestern University Press, Evanston, IL.

Cohen, R. and Uphoff, N. (1979) *Feasibility and Application of Rural*

Development Participation: A state of the art paper, Cornell University Press, Ithaca, NY.

Coleman, G. (1987a) 'Logical framework approach to the monitoring and evaluation of agricultural and rural development projects', *Project Appraisal*, Vol.2, No.4, pp.251–59.

Coleman, G. (1987b) 'Monitoring a rural credit project in Ethiopia', *Agricultural Administration and Extension*, Vol.24, No.2, pp.107–27.

Collinson, M. (1972) 'Conclusions on survey organisation and design', In *Farm Management in Peasant Agriculture*, Praeger, New York.

Collinson, M. (1988) 'The development of African farming systems: Some personal views', *Agricultural Administration and Extension*, Vol.29, pp.7–22.

Colson, E.F. (1960) *Social Organisation of the Gwembe Tonga*, Manchester University Press, Manchester.

Colson, E.F. (1971) *The Social Consequences of Resettlement*, Manchester University Press, Manchester.

Conway, G.R. (1985) 'Agroecosystem analysis', *Agricultural Administration*, Vol.20, pp.31–55.

Conyers, D. (1982) *An Introduction to Social Planning in the Third World*, John Wiley, New York.

Cook, T.D. and Reichardt, C.S. (eds) (1979) *Qualitative and Quantitative Methods in Evaluation Research*, Sage, London.

Copestake, J.G. (1988a) 'The transition to social banking in India: Promises and pitfalls', *Development Policy Review*, Vol.6, No.2, pp.139–64.

Copestake, J.G. (1988b) 'Refinancing rural development in India: A preliminary assessment of the National Bank For Agriculture and Rural Development (NABARD)', *Manchester Papers on Development*, Vol.4, No.2, pp.189–225.

Copestake, J.G., Thiele, G. and Farrington, J. (1987) 'The adulteration of coffee in Bolivia', *Tropical Science*, Vol.26, pp.129–34 .

Culture and Agriculture (1988) *Special Methods Issue*, Bulletin of Culture and Agriculture Group, Dept of Human Ecology, Rutgers University.

Dahl, G. (1979) *Suffering Grass*, University of Stockholm, Stockholm.

Damodaram, K. (1991) 'Measuring social development through development of qualitative indicators', *Community Development Journal*, Vol.26, No.4, pp.286–94.

Dedijer, S. and Jequier, N. (eds) (1987) *Intelligence for Economic Development*, BERG, Oxford.

Densham, P. and Rushton, G. (1988) 'Decision support systems for locational planning', In R.G. Golledge and H. Timmermans (eds) *Behavioural Modelling in Geography and Planning*, Croom Helm, London.

Denzin, N.K. (1970) *The Research Act*, Aldine, Chicago, IL.

Derman, W. and Whiteford, S. (eds) (1985) *Social Impact Analysis and Development Planning in the Third World*, Westview Press, Boulder, CO.

Devereux, S. and Hoddinott, J. (eds) (1993) *Fieldwork in Developing Countries*, Lynne Rienner, Boulder, CO.

Deyhle, D., Hess, D.A. and LeCompte, M. (1992) 'Approaching ethical issues for qualitative researchers in education'. In M. LeCompte *et al.* (eds) *The Handbook of Qualitative Research in Education*, Academic Press, London.

Duffield, M. (1993) 'Disaster relief and asset transfer in the Horn: political survival in a permanent emergency.' *Development and Change*, vol.24, pp.131-57.

Eder, J.F. (1982) *Who Shall Succeed? Agricultural development and social inequality on a Philippine frontier*, Cambridge University Press, Cambridge.

Ellen, R. (1984) *Ethnographic Research: A guide to general conduct*, Academic Press, London.

Farrington, J. (ed.) (1988) 'Farmer participatory research: editorial introduction', *Experimental Agriculture*, Vol.24, Part 3.

Farrington, J. and Martin, A. (1987) 'Farmer participatory research: A review of concepts and practices.' Agricultural Administration (research and extension) *Network paper*, No.19. Overseas Development Institute, London.

Feldstein, H.S. and Poats, S.V. (1989) 'Conceptual framework for gender analysis in farming systems research and extension', In H.S. Feldstein and S.V. Poats (eds) *Working Together: Vol.1: Case studies*, Kumarian Press, West Hartford, CT.

Fielding, N.S. and Fielding, J.L. (1986) *Linking Data. SAGE Qualitative research methods*, 2, Sage, Beverly Hills, CA.

Filstead, W.J. (1979) 'Qualitative Methods: A needed perspective in evaluation research', In T. Cook and C. Reichardt (eds) *Qualitative and Quantitative Methods in Evaluation Research*, Sage, Beverly Hills, CA.

Finch, J. (1986) 'Research and policy: the uses of qualitative methods in social and educational research', *Social research and educational studies series*, No. 2, The Falmer Press, Lewes and Philadelphia.

Finsterbusch, K. and Motz, A.B. (1980) *Social Research for Policy Decisions*, Wadsworth, Belmont, CA.

Finsterbusch, K. and van Wicklin III, W.A. (1989) 'Beneficiary participation in development projects: Empirical tests of popular theories', *Economic Development and Cultural Change*, Vol.37, No.3, pp.573–93.

Finsterbusch, K., Ingersoll, J., and Llewellyn, L. (eds) (1990) *Methods for Social Analysis in Developing Countries*, Westview Press, Boulder, CO.

Food and Agriculture Organisation of the United Nations (1986) *Guidelines for Designing Development Projects to Benefit the Rural Poor*, FAO, Rome.

Fowler, F.J. (1993) *Survey Research Methods*, Sage, Newbury Park, CA.

Frankenberger, T.R. (1991) 'Rapid food security assessment'. Paper presented at a workshop on famine mitigation, Tucson, Arizona, May 1991.

Franklin, J. and Thrasher, J. (1976) *An Introduction to Program Evaluation*, John Wiley, New York.

Franzel, S. and Crawford, E.W. (1987) 'Comparing formal and informal survey techniques for farming systems research: A case study from Kenya', *Agricultural Administration and Extension*, Vol.27, No.1, pp.13–34.

Freire, P. (1970) *Pedagogy of the Oppressed*, The Sedbury Press, New York.

Galaty, J., Aronson, D., and Salzman, P. (eds) (1981) *The Future of Pastoral Peoples*, IDRC, Ottawa.

Glaser, B.G. and Strauss, A.L. (1967) *The Discovery of Grounded Theory: Strategies for qualitative research*, Aldine de Gruyter, New York.

Glassner, B. and Moreno, J.D. (eds) (1989) *The Qualitative-quantitative Distinction in the Social Sciences*, Kluwer, London.

Grandin, B.E. (1987) *Wealth Ranking in Smallholder Communities: A field manual*, IT Publications, London.

Green, D.A.G. and Maddock, N. (1987) 'Facts for planning rural development: Some lessons in the administration of data collection from Malawi', *Agricultural Administration and Extension*, Vol.24, pp.33–48.

Greenwood, D. (1976) *Unrewarding wealth, the commercialisation and collapse of agriculture in a Spanish Basque town*, Cambridge University Press, Cambridge.

Gregory, C. and Altman, J. (1989) *Observing the Economy*, Routledge, London.

Gummesson, E. (1988) *Qualitative Methods in Management Research*, Chartwell-Bratt Ltd, Bromley.

Haberman, S.J. (1979) *Analysis of Qualitative Data*, Academic Press, New York and London.

Hansen, A. and Oliver-Smith, A. (1982) *Involuntary Migration and Resettlement: The problems and responses of dislocated peoples*, Westview Press, Boulder, CO.

Harding, P. (1991) 'Qualitative indicators and the project framework', *Community Development Journal*, Vol.26, No.4, pp.294–306.

Harvey, J., Potten, D.H. and Schoppmann, B. (1987) 'Rapid rural appraisal of small irrigation schemes in Zimbabwe', *Agricultural Administration and Extension*, Vol.27, No.3, pp.141–56.

Heginbotham, S.J. (1975) *Cultures in Conflict: The four faces of Indian bureaucracy*, Columbia University Press, Columbia, NY.

Heyer, J., Ireri, D. and Moris, J. (1971) *Rural Development in Kenya*, East African Publishing House, Nairobi.

Hildebrand, P. (1981) 'Combining disciplines in rapid appraisal: The Sondeo approach', *Agricultural Administration*, Vol.8, pp.423–32.

Hoare, P.W.C. and Crouch, B.R. (1988) 'Required changes to the project management cycle to facilitate participatory rural development', *Agricultural Administration and Extension*, Vol.30, No.1.

Hocksbergen, R. (1986) 'Approaches to evaluation of development interventions: The importance of world and life views', *World Development*, Vol.14, No.2, pp.283–300.

Hoddinott, J. (1933) 'Fieldwork under time constraints', In S. Devereux and J. Hoddinott (eds) (1993) *Fieldwork in Developing Countries*, Lynne Rienner, Boulder, CO.

Hoeper, B. (ed.) (1990) *Qualitative "versus" quantitative approaches in applied empirical research in rural development*, Proceedings of a workshop at Sokoine University of Agriculture in Morogoro, Tanzania. German Foundation for International Development (DSE), Bonn.

Honadle, G. (1982) 'Rapid reconnaissance for development administration', *World Development*, Vol.10, No.8, pp.633–49.

House, P.W. and Shull, R.D. (1991) *The Practice of Policy Analysis: Forty years of art and technology*, The Compass Press, Washington DC.

Howes, M. (1991) 'Linking paradigms and practice: Key issues in the appraisal, monitoring and evaluation of British NGO projects'. Paper presented at the 1991 Development Studies Association Conference, Swansea, September 1991.

Hursch-Cesar, G. and Roy, P. (1976) *Third World Surveys: Survey research in developing nations*, Macmillan of India, Delhi.

Ianni, F.A.J. and Orr, M.T. (1979) 'Toward a rapprochement of quantitative and qualitative methodologies', In T. Cook and C. Reichardt (eds) *Qualitative and Quantitative Methods in Evaluation Research*, Sage, Beverly Hills, CA.

IIED/MYRADA (1991) 'Participatory rural appraisal: Proceedings of the February 1991 Bangalore PRA trainers workshop', *RRA Notes* No.13, IIED, London.

Ilchman, W. (1972) 'Decision rules and decision roles', *The African Review*, Vol.2, pp.219–46.

Jain, R.K., Urban, L.V., Stacey, G.S. and Balbach, H.E. (1993) *Environmental Assessment*, McGraw-Hill, New York.

Johnson, J.M. (1975) *Doing Field Research*, The Free Press, New York.

Judd, C.M. and Kenny, D.A. (1981) 'The post-only correlational design', In *Estimating the Effects of Social Interventions*, Cambridge University Press, Cambridge.

Kearl, B. (ed.) (1976) *Field Data Collection in the Social Sciences: Experiences in Africa and the Middle East*, Agricultural Development Council, New York.

Keller, J. (1990) 'A holistic approach to irrigation scheme water management', In R.K. Sampath and R.A. Young (eds) (1990) *Social, Economic, and Institutional Issues in Third World Irrigation Management*, Westview Press, Boulder, CO.

Kesseba, A.M. (ed.) (1989) *Technology Systems for Small Farmers: Issues and options*, Westview Press with the International Fund for Agricultural Development, Boulder, CO.

Keregero, K.J.B. and Keregero, M.M. (1990) 'Participatory action research: Enabling scientists to empower the rural poor', In B. Hoeper (ed) (1990) *Qualitative "versus" quantitative approaches in applied empirical research in rural development*, Proceedings of a workshop at Sokoine University of Agriculture in Morogoro, Tanzania. German Foundation for International Development (DSE), Bonn.

Khon Kaen University (Faculty of Agriculture) (1987) *Proceedings of the 1985 International Conference on Rapid Rural Appraisal*, Bureau for Science and Technology, USAID, Washington DC.

Korten, D.C. (1987) 'Third generation NGO strategies: A key to people-centred development', *World Development*, Vol.15, Supplement, pp.145–60.

Kottach, C.R. (1991) 'When people don't come first: Some sociological lessons from completed projects', In M.M. Cernea (ed) (1991) *Putting People First: Sociological variables in rural development*, Oxford University Press for the World Bank, New York.

Kuhn, T.S. (1970) *The Structure of Scientific Revolutions*, University of Chicago Press, Chicago, IL.

Kuik, O.J., Oosterhuis, F.H., Jansen, H.M.A., Holm, K. and Ewers, H.J. (1992) *Assessment of Benefits of Environmental Measures*, Graham and Trotman, London.

Kumar, K. (1987) *A Manager's Guide to Rapid, Low-cost Data Collection Methods*, USAID, Washington DC.

Lancy, D.F. (1993) *Qualitative Research in Education: An introduction to the major traditions*, Longman, London.

Latham, M.C. (1972) *Planning and evaluation of applied nutrition programmes,* FAO, Rome.

LeCompte, M.D., Millroy, W. and Preissle, J. (eds) (1993) *The Handbook of Qualitative Research in Education,* Academic Press, London.

Leistritz, F.L. and Murdock, S.H. (1981) *The Socioeconomic Impact of Resource Assessment: Methods of assessment,* Westview Press, Boulder CO.

Leiter, K. (1980) *A Primer on Ethnomethodology,* Oxford, New York.

Lewis, D.J. (1993) 'Going it alone: female-headed households, rights and resources in rural Bangladesh', *Centre for Development Studies, Bath University, Occasional Paper* 01/93.

Lidz, C. (1989) '"Objectivity" and rapport', In B. Glassner and J.D. Moreno (eds) (1989) *The Qualitative-quantitative Distinction in the Social Sciences,* Kluwer, London, pp.43–56.

Lightfoot, C. and Barker, R. (1988) 'On-farm trials: A survey of methods.' *Agricultural Administration and Extension,* Vol.30, No.1, pp.15–23.

Lincoln, Y. and Guba, E. (1985) *Naturalistic Inquiry,* Sage, Beverly Hills, CA.

Lockwood, M. (1993) 'Facts or fictions? Fieldwork relationships and the nature of data', In S. Devereux and J. Hoddinott (eds) (1993) *Fieldwork in Developing Countries,* Lynne Reinner, Boulder, CO.

Longhurst, R. (1981) 'Research methodology and rural economy in northern Nigeria', *IDS Bulletin,* Vol.12, No.4, pp.23–31.

Marsden, D. and Oakley, P. (eds) (1990) 'Evaluating social development projects.' *OXFAM Development Guidelines,* No.5, Oxfam, Oxford.

Maxwell, S. (1984a) 'The social scientist in farming systems research', *Discussion Paper* 199-II, IDS, Sussex.

Maxwell, S. (1984b) 'The role of case studies in farming systems research', *Discussion Paper* 198-II, IDS, Sussex.

Maxwell, S. (1984c) 'Farming systems research: Hitting a moving target', *Discussion Paper* 199-I, IDS, Sussex.

McCracken, G. (1988) 'The long interview', *Qualitative Research Methods Series 13,* Sage, Newbury Park, CA.

McCracken, J.A., Pretty, J.N. and Conway, G.R. (1988) *An Introduction to Rapid Rural Appraisal for Agricultural Development,* International Institute for Environment and Development, London.

McGaw, B. (1981) 'Exploratory Data Analysis', In N.L. Smith (ed.) *New Techniques for Evaluation,* Sage, Beverley Hills.

Mickelwait, D.R. (1979) 'Information strategies for implementing rural development.' In: G. Honadle and R. Klauss (eds) *International Development Administration,* Praeger, New York.

Miles, B.M. and Huberman, A.M. (1984) *Qualitative Data Analysis: A sourcebook of new methods,* Sage, Beverley Hills, CA.

Mintzberg, H. (1973) *The Nature of Managerial Work,* Harper and Row, New York.

Molnar, A. (1989) *A Review of Rapid Appraisal Tools for Use in Natural Resource Management Planning and Project Design and Execution,* FAO Forest Department, Rome.

Monke, E. and Pearson, S. (1989) *The Policy Analysis Matrix for Agricultural Development,* Cornell University Press, Ithaca, NY.

Moock, J.L. (ed.) (1986) *Understanding Africa's Rural Households and Farming Systems*, Westview Press, Boulder CO.

Moran, E.F. (1981) *Developing the Amazon*, Indiana University Press, Bloomington, Indiana.

Morgan, D.L. (1991) *Focus Groups as Qualitative Research*, Sage, Newbury Park, CA.

Moris, J. (1970) *The Agrarian Revolution in Central Kenya: A study of farm innovation in Embu district*, Northwestern University, Evanston, IL.

Moris, J. (1984) *Institutional Choice for Rural Development*, Harvard Institute for International Development, Cambridge, MA.

Moris, J. (1991) *Extension Alternatives in Tropical Africa*, Overseas Development Institute, London.

Naroll, R. (1962) *Data Quality Control – A new research technique*, The Free Press of Glencoe, New York.

Norman, D., Simmons, E. and Hays, H. (1982) *Farming Systems in the Nigerian Savanna*, Westview Press, Boulder, Co.

Oakley, P. (1988) 'Conceptual problems of the monitoring and evaluation of qualitative objectives of rural development', *Community Development Journal*, Vol.23, No.1, pp.3–11.

O'Barr, W.M., Spain, D.H. and Tessler, M.A. (eds) (1973) *Survey Research in Africa*, Northwestern University Press, Evanston, IL.

Overholt, C.A., Cloud, K., Anderson, M.B. and Austin, J. (1991) 'Gender analysis framework', In A. Rao, M.B. Anderson, and C.A. Overholt (eds) *Gender Analysis in Development Planning*, Kumarian Press, Hartford, CT.

Patton, C.V. and Sawicki, D. (1986) *Basic Methods of Policy Analysis and Planning*, Prentice-Hall, Englewood Cliffs, NJ.

Patton, M.Q. (1980) *Qualitative Evaluation Methods*, Sage, Beverley Hills, CA.

Patton, M.Q. (1987) *How to Use Qualitative Methods in Evaluation*, Sage, Newbury Park, CA.

Patton, M.Q. (1990) *Qualitative Evaluation and Research Methods*, Sage 2nd edition, Newbury Park, CA.

Peuse, H.G. and Mbaga, W.D.S. (1987) 'Helping farm groups problem-solve: A workshop macrodesign for extension workers', *Agricultural Administration and Extension*, Vol.26, No.1, pp.17–25.

Pratt, B. and Boyden, J. (eds) (1985) *The Field Directors' Handbook: An Oxfam manual for development workers*, Oxford University Press for Oxfam, Oxford.

Rahman, Anisur. (1992) *People's Self-Development*, Zed Books, London.

Reason, P. (ed.) (1988) *Human Inquiry in Action*, Sage, London.

Rhoades, R.E. (1982) *The Art of the Informal Agricultural Survey*, International Potato Centre, Lima.

Rhoades, R.E. (1984) *Breaking New Ground: Agricultural anthropology*, International Potato Centre, Lima.

Rhoades, R.E. (1985) 'Informal survey methods for farming systems research', *Human Organisation*, Vol.44, No.3, pp.215–18.

Rhoades, R.E. and Booth, R. (1982) 'Farmer-back-to-farmer: A model for generating acceptable agricultural technology', *Agricultural Administration*, Vol.11, pp.127–37.

Richards, P. (1985) *Indigenous Agricultural Revolution*, Hutchinson, London.

Riddell, R. and Robinson, M. (1992) *Evaluating NGO Performance: Existing studies and the ODI approach*, ODI Unpublished working paper, Overseas Development Institute, London.

Rogers, E.M. (1983) *Diffusion of Innovations*, Collier Macmillan, London.

Rondinelli, D. (1983) *Development Projects as Policy Experiments*, Methuen, London.

Saasa, O. (1985) 'Public policy-making in developing countries: The utility of contemporary decision-making models', *Public Administration and Development*, Vol.5, No.4, pp.309–21.

Salmen, L.F. (1987) *Listen to People: Participant-observer evaluation of development projects*, Oxford University Press for the World Bank, Oxford.

Sampath, R.K. and Young, R.A. (eds) (1990) *Social, Economic, and Institutional Issues in Third World Irrigation Management*, Westview Press, Boulder CO.

Santo Pietro, D. (ed.) (1983) *Evaluation Sourcebook*, American committee of voluntary agencies for foreign service.

Schensul, J. and Schensul, S. (1992) 'Collaborative research: Methods of inquiry for social change', In M. Lecompte, W. Millroy, and J. Preissle (eds) (1993) *The Handbook of Qualitative Research in Education*, Academic Press, London.

Scott, R.A. and Shore, A.R. (1979) *Why Sociology Does Not Apply: A study of the use of sociology in public policy*, Elsevier, New York.

Scudder, T. (1982) *From Welfare to Development: A conceptual framework for the analysis of dislocated peoples*, Hansen and Oliver-Smith.

Sen, B. (1987) 'NGO Self-evaluation: Issues of concern', *World Development*, Vol.15, Supplement, pp.161–68.

Shaner, W.W., Philipp, P.F. and Schmel, W.R. (1982) *Farming Systems Research and Development*, Westview Press, Boulder CO.

Simmonds, N.W. (1985) 'Farming Systems Research: A review', *World Bank Technical Paper*, No.43, World Bank, Washington, DC.

Smith, W., Lethem, F. and Thoolen, B. (1980) *The Design of Organisations for Rural Development*, The World Bank, Washington, DC.

Soderstrom, E.J. (1981) *Social Impact Assessment*, Praeger, New York.

Stewart, I. (1986) 'Response farming: A scientific approach to ending starvation and alleviating poverty in drought zones of Africa', In Y.T. Moses (ed.) *Proceedings, African Agricultural Development Conference: Technology, Ecology and Society*, California State Polytechnic University, Pomona, CA.

Stonecash, J. (1980) 'Politics, wealth and public policy: The significance of political systems', In T.R. Dye and V. Gray (eds) *The Determinants of Public Policy*, Heath, Toronto.

Streiffeler, F. (1990) 'Qualitative "versus" quantitative methods in social research', In B. Hoeper (ed.) (1990) *Qualitative "versus" quantitative approaches in applied empirical research in rural development*, Proceedings of a workshop at Sokoine University of Agriculture in Morogoro, Tanzania, German Foundation for International Development (DSE), Bonn.

Stull, D. and Schensul, J. (eds) (1987) *Collaborative Research and Social Change*, Westview Press, Boulder CO.

Suchman, E.A. (1967) *Evaluation Research*, Russell Sage, New York.

Sutherland, A. (1987) 'Sociology in farming systems research', Agricultural Administration Unit *Occasional Paper* 6, ODI, London.

Therkildsen, O. (1988) *Watering White Elephants?*, Scandinavian Institute of African Studies, Uppsala.

Trend, M.G. (1978) 'On the reconciliation of qualitative and quantitative analysis: A case study', *Human Organisation*, Vol.37, No.4, pp.345–54.

Tripp, R. (1982) 'Data collection, site selection and farmer participation in on-farm experimentation,' CIMMYT, Economics program, Working paper 82/1.

Trow, M. (1957) 'Comment on participant observation and interviewing: A comparison', *Human Organisation*, Vol.16, pp.33–35.

Tukey, J.W. (1977) *Exploratory Data Analysis*, Addison-Wesley, Reading, MA.

UNRISD (1990) 'Qualitative indicators of development', *Discussion Paper* 15, UNRISD, Geneva.

UNRISD (1991) *Qualitative Indicators and Development Data: Current concerns and priorities*, UNRISD, Geneva.

Uphoff, N. (1988) 'Participatory evaluation of farmer organisations' capacity for development tasks', *Agricultural Administration and Extension*, Vol.30, pp.43–64.

Uphoff, N. (1990) 'Paraprojects as new modes of international development assistance', *World Development*, Vol.18, No.10, pp.1401–11.

Uphoff, N. (1991) 'A field methodology for participatory self-evaluation', *Community Development Journal*, Vol.26, No.4, pp.271–85.

Uphoff, N. (1991) 'Fitting projects to people', In M.M. Cernea (ed.) (1991) *Putting People First: Sociological variables in rural development*, Oxford University Press for the World Bank, New York.

Van Maanen, J. (1979) 'The fact of fiction in organisational ethnography', *Administrative Science Quarterly*, Vol.24, No.4, pp.539–50.

Van Maanen, J. (1983) *Qualitative Methodology*, Sage, Beverley Hills, CA.

Vulliamy, G., Lewin, K. and Stephens, D. (1990) 'Doing educational research in developing countries', *Social research and educational studies series*, No. 9, The Falmer Press, Lewes and Philadelphia.

Wainer, H. (ed.) (1986) *Drawing Inferences from Self-Selection Samples*, Springer Verlag, New York.

Warren, C.A. (1988) *Gender Issues in Field Research*, Sage, Newbury Park, CA.

Wengle, J.L. (1988) *Ethnographers in the Field: The psychology of research*, University of Alabama Press, London.

Weiss, C.H. (1972) *Evaluation Research*, Prentice-Hall, Englewood Cliffs, NJ.

Wellard, K. and Copestake, J.G. (1993) *Non-Governmental Organisations and the State in Africa: Rethinking Roles in Sustainable Agricultural Development*, Routledge, London.

White, L.G. (1990) *Implementing Policy Reforms in LDCs*, Lynne Reinner, Boulder, CO.

Whyte, A.V. (1977) 'Guidelines for field studies in environmental perception.' *MAB Technical Notes*, UNESCO, Paris.

Whyte, W.F. (1989) *Learning from the Field: a guide from experience*, Sage, Newbury Park, CA.

Whyte, W.F. (1991) *Social Theory for Action*, Sage, Newbury Park, CA.

Wiggins, S. (1992) 'Against the odds: Managing agricultural projects in Africa: Evidence from Sierra Leone and Zambia', *International Review of Administrative Sciences*, Vol.58, pp.79–92.

Wilson, F. (1983) 'Monitoring small farm credit', *Agricultural Administration*, Vol.14, No.4, pp.191–202.

Wilson, K. and Morren, G.E.B (1990) *Systems Approaches for Improvement in Agriculture and Resource Management*, Collier Macmillan, London.

Wilson, K. (1993) 'Thinking about the ethics of fieldwork', In S. Devereux and J. Hoddinott (eds) (1993) *Fieldwork in Developing Countries*, Lynne Reinner, Boulder, CO.

Wolcott, H.F. (1990) *Writing Up Qualitative Research*, Sage, Newbury Park, CA.

Wood, G.D. and Palmer-Jones, R. (1991) *The Water Sellers: A co-operative venture by the rural poor*, IT Publications, London.

World Bank (1991) 'The social dimensions of adjustment priority survey; An instrument for the rapid identification and monitoring of policy target groups', Social Dimensions of Adjustment in Sub-Saharan Africa, Working Paper No.12.

Wotowiec, P. Jr, Poats, S.V. and Hildebrand, P.E. (1988) 'Research, recommendation and diffusion domains: A farming systems approach to targeting', In S.V. Poats, M. Schmink and A. Spring (eds) *Gender Issues in Farming Systems Research and Extension*, Westview Press, Boulder CO.

Yin, R.K. (1984) 'Case study research: Design and Methods', *Applied social research methods series*, Vol.5. Sage, Beverley Hills, CA.

Young, F.W. (1982) 'A practical methodology for evaluating integrated rural development', *Sociologia Ruralis*, Vol.22, No.3/4, pp.293–304 .

Young, F.W., Bertoli, F. and Bertoli, S. (1981a) 'Design for a microcomputer-based rural development information system', *Social Indicators Research*, Vol.9, pp.283–312.

Young, F.W., Bertoli, F. and Bertoli, S. (1981b) 'Rural poverty and ecological problems: Results of a new type of baseline study', *Social Indicators Research*, Vol.9, pp.495–516.

Zaltman, G., Pinson, C. and Angelmar, R. (1973) *Metatheory and Consumer Research*, Holt, Rinehart and Winston, New York.

Zandstra, H. et al. (1979) *Caqueza: Living rural development*, International Development Research Center, Ottawa.

Zich, J. (1990) 'Some critical aspects in gathering socio-economic data in rural areas of non-western societies', In B. Hoeper (ed.) (1990) *Qualitative "versus" quantitative approaches in applied empirical research in rural development*, Proceedings of a workshop at Sokoine University of Agriculture in Morogoro, Tanzania, German Foundation for International Development (DSE), Bonn.

Index

action research v, 54, 62, 73, 94
administrative staff 11
advanced planning 53, 60
Africa 16, 25, 31, 45, 52, 60, 61, 69,
    71, 78
  Sub-Saharan 25, 45
agency v, vii, 10, 14, 20, 25-27, 26,
    28, 29, 31, 33, 34, 48, 49, 54, 62,
    78, 80
  coverage 3, 12, 25, 68, 79, 80, 90, 94
  features 29, 32
  internal workings 26, 29
  morale 25, 29, 79, 80
  reliability 7, 11, 25, 31, 45, 47, 55,
    79, 80, 88, 90, 92
  speciality 26
agency-level variables 20
agribusiness 74
agricultural extension 13, 17, 79, 78
  extension workers 17,61 79
  Training & Visit 17
agricultural research vi, vii, 2, 3, 13,
    16, 39, 40, 45, 62, 67-70, 72, 73
  orthodox agricultural research vii,
    68, 70, 72
  multidisciplinary 38, 52, 54, 61,
    70, 72
  research station 68
agro-ecology 57
agroforestry 62
aid agencies 80
AIDS 96
Amazon 60
Anderson International Associates 84
anecdotal material 87
animal husbandry 9
anti-projects 75
Argyris, C. 36
Arnon, I. 67
Baker, D. 73
Bangladesh 62
Bangladesh Rural Advancement
Committee 39
2 banks 14, 17, 83
  borrower appraisal 83

branch performance 83
  rural banking 14, 17
  banking operations 83
Bardeere dam 34
Barker, R. 62, 70
Barlett, P. 45, 60
Belshaw, D.G.R. 69, 78
beneficiaries 32, 41, 43, 74, 75, 86
Berdegué, J.A. 73
bias 6, 28, 47-49, 55, 74, 75
Biggs, S.D. viii, 7, 50
biotechnology 71
blueprint approach 74
Bolivia vii, 81, 82
Booth, D. 38, 73
Boyden, J. 40, 42
BRAC see: Bangladesh Rural
    Advancement Committee
Branch, K. 44, 83
Braun, G. 75
Brewer, R.J. 37, 42
Brown, D. 42
budget 13, 22, 74
Bunch, R. 73
bureaucracies 52, 73-75, 91, 92
Burgess, R.G. 38
Buse, R.C. 93
Cairncross, S. 33, 78
case study 47, 78
cash income 31
Casley, D.J. 1, 17, 20, 37, 54, 58
CDR (complex, diverse and risky)
    68-70, 73
Cernea, M.M. viii, 18, 38, 71
CGIAR see: Consultative Group on
    International Agricultural Research

Chambers, R. viii, 37, 38, 55, 63,
    67-69, 73, 75
Chandramouli, K. 84
channels of information 12
China 34
civil engineers 78
CIMMYT see: International Maize
    and Wheat Research Centre

111

Clayton, E. 20
coca 77
coffee vii, 82
Coffee Board 82
Cohen, R. 3
Coleman, G. 34, 76, 75
collective responsibility 43, 61
Collinson, M. viii, 38, 39, 69, 72
colonial period 90
Colson, E.F. 60
commodity prices 20
communities v, vii, 10, 11, 25, 28,
    30-32, 39-42, 48, 55, 59, 61, 62,
    76, 77-80, 89
  involvement of 33
  in conflict 40
  community leaders 10, 55, 61
  community traits 30
  community-level variation 11
Community Development Journal 42
comparative study 24
computers 23, 54, 95, 97
constraints analysis 16
construction projects 26, 29
consultants 23, 54, 55, 88
Consultative Group on International
Agricultural Research 70
consumer sovereignty 74
contacts 17, 20, 55, 56, 68, 82
contemporary trends vi, 3, 93
Conway, G.R. 39, 40, 58, 73, 96
Conyers, D. 44, 78
Cook, T.D. 36, 48
Copestake, J.G. iii, viii, 17, 62, 82, 83
corruption vii, 24, 29, 31, 87
cost pricing 29
cost-based monitoring 74
cost-effectiveness 20, 45, 48, 97
Coulter, J.K. 71
Crawford, E.W. 7, 50, 88
credit vi, vii, 17, 26, 32, 49, 60,
    81-83, 85
  programmes vi, 26, 83
  relations 81
crop yields 8, 16, 30
Crouch, B.R. 74
cultural expectation 51
Dahl, G. 60
Damodaram, K. 42
Dar es Salaam 65
data vii, 3, 4, 44, 48, 52, 53, 80, 93,
    94
  bad data vii, 52

observational data 4
official price data 80
primary data 3
raw data 44
subsidiary data 94
variable data 53
data bases 48, 93
debt collection 83
decentralization 12, 74, 75
Dedijer, S. 63
delegation of decisions 12
demand-pull 74
Denzin, N.K. 46, 47
dependency syndrome 30
Derman, W. 44
developing countries 6
  rural development 1, iii, 1-3, 6, 9,
    10, 9, 12, 15, 20, 21, 24, 26,
    29, 32, 35, 36, 38, 39,
    42-45, 47, 54, 55, 57, 59,
    63, 64, 74, 88, 93, 94, 95,
    97
  rural development tourism 38, 55,
    57
  social development v, 23, 40-43,
    75
Devereux, S. 37, 54, 58, 81
diagnosis 16-18, 23, 40, 70-73
diagnostic surveys 71, 72
direct cash housing allowance 47
disaster vi, 2, 14, 84, 96
disaster response vi, 2, 14, 84, 96
diversity 9, 45, 46, 57, 71, 74, 89, 91
donor 13, 19, 22, 33, 35, 73, 75, 77,
    84
Driscoll, J.L. 93
drought vii, 14, 64, 65, 64, 66, 68,
    84, 89
Duffield, M. 96
early warning systems 84
economies of scale 74
Eder, J.F. 60
education vii, 9, 11, 13, 38, 79, 78,
    80
  education policy 38
  educational research 47
Embu vii, 48
enquiry, rural 9, 15, 25, 34, 39, 45, 61,
    67, 68, 73, 81, 92
  enquiry, empirical 80
epistemology 3, 47
ethnography 60
evaluation v, vii, 2, 9, 13, 17, 16, 23,

112

24, 30, 34, 35, 38, 40-45, 60, 62, 69, 70, 80, 94
external surveillance 20
factionalism 11, 30, 31
factory environment 20
FAO see: Food and Agriculture Organisation
farm 9, 11, 13, 30-32, 34, 45, 50, 57, 59, 61, 62, 67, 70-73, 78
farm-level variation 11
farm management surveys 45
farmer vi, 11, 39, 40, 45, 50, 57, 59, 60, 62, 67, 68, 70, 72-74, 79, 92
farmer first and last (FFL) 67
farmer support services 79
farmer training 60, 92
farmer's income 11
farmers' key goals 72
farming calendar 60
farming, peasant 71
farming practices 11
farming systems vi, 3, 7, 16, 38, 67-73, 96
farming systems homogenous 69
farming systems research (FSR) 16, 38, 61, 67, 69-74
progressive farmers 55
Farrington, J. viii, 68, 73, 74
female stock 64
FFL see: farmer first and last
Fielding, N.S. 36, 50
Fielding, J.L.
field work 10, 53, 54, 60, 90
fieldwork strategies vii, 37
field staff 10, 21, 22, 25, 28, 30, 33, 50, 52, 62, 90
field survey 22, 30
field units 14, 21, 28
field workshops 61
financial goals 83
financial institutions 83
financiers 97
Finch, J. 38
Finsterbusch, K. 41-44, 96
focus groups 37, 40, 60
food balance 84
Food and Agriculture Organisation viii, 43, 54, 74
formal survey 50
formal training 90
Fowler, F.J. 58
framework vii, 3, 15, 45, 53, 76, 75,

76
Frankenberger, T.R. 84, 85
Franzel, J. 7, 50, 88
FSR see: farming systems research 90
funding organizations 21
Galaty, J. 60
geographic information systems 93, 94
GIS see: geographic information systems
Glaser, B.G. 3, 36
goals 9, 17, 18, 23, 24, 34, 39, 41, 62, 72, 75, 76, 83
Grandin, B.E. 31, 89
Greenwood, D. 60
group discussions 36, 54, 76
Guatemala 69
Haberman, S.J. 4, 36
Hall, M. viii, 69
Harding, P. 42, 76
Harvey, J. 57, 75
health vii, 9, 13, 17, 79, 78, 80, 85
high income countries 20
Hildebrand, P. 38, 61, 67, 69, 71
historical perspective 58
Hoare, P.W.C. 74
Hocksbergen, R. 44
Hoddinott, J. 37, 54, 58, 81
holistic 34, 54, 60, 69, 71
Honadle, G. 38
House, P.W. 27, 56, 63, 90, 93
Howes, M. viii, 43, 44
Hunter, A. 37, 42
Hursh-Cesar, G. 37, 58
Ianni, F.A.J. 47
IIED see: International Institute for Environment and Development
ILCA see: International Livestock Centre for Africa
Ilchman, W. 39
indebtedness 11, 31, 60
India 17, 60, 83
indicators 3, 7, 8, 26, 29, 42, 57, 63-65, 64, 76, 75, 83, 85, 84
key 64
non-economic 8
social 8
indigenous technical knowledge 40, 43
individual ignorance 88, 90
information 4, 6, 20, 29, 34, 35, 67, 75
informal 20, 29
information handling 4, 35

information technology 35
information-systems 75
recorded information 6
rural information 6, 34, 67
informants v, vi, 3, 24, 34, 36, 40, 48,
   50, 53, 54, 56-58, 63, 65, 78, 81,
   86, 88
   informants, key v, vi, 3, 24, 34, 36,
      40, 48, 50, 53, 54, 56, 58, 63,
      65, 78, 81, 86, 88
infrastructure vi, 2, 13, 31, 77, 78, 80
Ingersoll, J. 96
intelligence work 63
intensive team visit 71
interest rates 20, 49, 83
International Institute for Environment
   and Development 40, 96
International Livestock Centre for Africa
70, 72
International Maize and Wheat Research
Centre 71
International Rice Research Institute 71
interpreter 5, 54, 59
interventionist 4
interventions vii, 16, 18, 23, 24, 29,
   30, 34, 46, 53, 62, 63, 70, 80, 81,
   91
   parallel interventions 53
investigator 3-5, 7, 18, 37, 48, 50, 53,
   54, 57-59, 86
IRRI see: International Rice Research
   Institute
irrigation scheme 60
ITK   see: indigenous   technical
   knowledge
Jequier, N. 63
Jiggins, J. 67
Johnson, J.M. 36
journalism 48, 53
Kearl, B. 37
Keller, J. 16, 71, 96
Kenya vii, 48, 60, 62
Kesseba, A.M. 68
Khon Kaen University 39
knowledge gaps 53, 55
Korten, D.C. 41, 43
Kuhn, T.S. 68
Kumar, K. 1, 17, 20, 37, 54, 58
labour   11, 16, 27, 31, 52, 72

   peak labour demand 52
Lancy, D.F. 3, 47
land-use 4, 71

large landowners 50
Latin America 77
learning-by-doing 74
LeCompte, M.D. 3
Leistritz, F.L. 44
Leiter, K. 36
Lethem, F. 26
Lewin, K. 47
Lewis, D.J. 96
Lightfoot, C. 62, 70
Llewellyn, L. 96
logical framework vii, 45, 76, 75, 76
Lury, D.A. 1
Maasai vii, 22, 65, 64, 66
management 2, 9, 13, 21, 24-26, 28,
   29, 31, 34-36, 45, 50, 71, 86, 91,
   93, 94, 97
management information systems
   35, 93, 94, 97
management of money 31
managerial control 29
managers 10, 19-21, 23, 28-30,
   49, 83, 87, 90, 97
MIS see management information
systems 94, 97
market 13, 49, 64, 80, 82, 85, 87
   marketing vi, vii, 2, 14, 26, 32,
      49, 65, 64, 77, 80, 81
   marketing chain 80
   marketing system 80
   rural marketing 14
Marsden, D. 23, 42
Martin, A. 68, 73, 74
mass media 10
mathematical analysis 1, 6
Maxwell, S. 69, 73
Mazingira institute 62
Mbaga, W.D.S. 61
McCracken, J.A. 37, 39, 40, 73, 96
McCracken, G. 58
measured coefficients 63
methodological pluralism v, 46, 47
micro-climates 11
middle income countries 21
Miles, P.M. 87
military conflict 14
Millroy, W. 3
Mintzberg, H. 12, 20
Molnar, A. 18, 75
monitoring systems 21, 23
Monke, E. 44
monopoly procurement 80
Moran, E.F. 60

Morgan, D.L. 37
Moris, J. iii, viii, 11, 16, 27, 48, 60
Morren, G.E.B. 68-70
Motz, A.B. 44
Murdock, S.H. 44
MYRADA see: Mysore Relief and Development Agency
Mysore Relief and Development Agency 40
Naroll, R. 51, 88
natural science 5, 47, 68, 69, 71
NGO see: non-governmental organization
Nigeria 69
Non-governmental organization vi, 62, 87, 89, 97
non-specialists 88
Norman, D. 69, 71
Nuer 86
O'Barr, W.M. 58
Oakley, P. 23, 42
official visit 55
opportunity analysis 16, 71, 96
organic farming 74
organizational variation 27
Orr, M.T. 47
outside investigator 57
ownership status 11
ox-blood 82
Oxfam 40, 42
Pacey, A. 68, 73
Palmer-Jones, R. 62
para-projects 75
participant observation v, 3, 36, 40, 46, 48, 54, 60
participatory planning 33
Participatory Rural Appraisal vi, 2, 40, 57, 73, 95, 96
pastoralism, Boran 60
Patton, C.V. 44
Patton, M.Q. 3, 23, 36, 37, 42, 46, 47, 54, 63, 94
Pearson, S. 44
performance reports 29
Peru 69
Peuse, H.G. 61
Philippines 60, 71
physical geography 56
pluralist approach 67
policy analysis v, 44, 45, 93
policy switch 54
policymakers 10, 42, 44, 61, 96
policymaking, rural 7, 39

political factors 32
political favouritism 77
PRA see: Participatory Rural Appraisal vi, 2, 40, 57, 73, 95, 96
practitioner 9
Pratt, B. viii, 40, 42
Preissle, J. 3
Pretty, J.N. 39, 40, 58, 73, 96
primary documentation 53
Private Voluntary Organisation vi, 97
procedural complexity 74
procedural inputs 18
programme designers 32
projects vi, vii, 15, 33, 35, 42, 45, 74, 75, 76, 94
    project cycle vi, vii, 15, 33, 35, 42, 45, 74, 75, 94
    project impact 76
    project spending 74
Proshika 62
proxy 21, 25, 75, 76
psychology 36
public accountability 75
public decisions 54
public investment 13
public sector reform 23
public sector services vi, 13, 78
public service departments 9
PVO see: Private Voluntary Organisation
qualitative v, vi, vii, 1-9, 15, 16, 18, 20-24, 29, 33-38, 40, 42, 44-48, 50, 49-54, 57, 58, 61-65, 64-67, 70-75, 77-81, 83-97
    approach 64
    dimensions 95
    enquiry v, vi, 1-4, 7-9, 15, 18, 21, 23, 24, 34, 36, 44-46, 48-53, 57, 58, 62-64, 67, 71-73, 75, 77, 79-81, 83-86, 88-94, 96, 97
    feedback 78
    indicators 7, 8, 65
    information 1, 4, 7, 88, 89, 91
    interpretation 24
    methods 1, 4, 23, 33, 35-38, 40, 42, 44, 46, 47, 70, 80, 86
    report 4, 47
    sources 4, 7, 61, 86-88
    work 53
quantitative 5, 15, 62
    approach 71
    data 4, 6, 7, 44, 77
    enquiry, formal 7
    measurement 75, 84

performance indicators 57
research vii, 5, 89
work 71
questionnaires 38, 39, 49, 50, 58, 61, 72, 89
pre-set questionnaires 58
range development 26
range scientist 4, 64
Rapid Food Security Assessment vii, 84, 85
Rapid Rural Appraisal v, vi, 2, 18, 38-40, 44, 57, 70, 73, 75, 81, 85, 88, 90, 96
Reason, P. 21, 28, 57, 61, 64, 82, 84, 95
recommendation domains 69, 72
reductionist 69
refugee 96
Reichardt, C.S. 36, 48
relief work 62
report writing 52, 53, 95
verbal reporting 53
resources 2, 11, 16, 18, 21, 25-27, 29, 38, 41, 47, 53, 64, 76, 80, 84, 86, 87, 93, 94, 97
allocation 69
availabilities 11
profiling 96
respondents vi, 3-5, 49, 51, 63, 65, 95
Rhoades, R.E. 38, 69, 73
Richards, P. 73
Riddell, R. 76
Robinson, M. 76
Rogers, E.M. 45
Rondonelli, D. 74
Roy, P. 37, 58
RRA see: Rapid Rural Appraisal
Russell, J.F.A. 71
Saasa, O. 19
Salmen, L.F. 54, 60
Sampath, R.K. 96
Santo Pietro, D. 23
Sawicki, D. 44, 63
scanning 19, 20
Scott, R.A. 36, 63
Scudder, T. 60, 78
self-reliance 7, 40
Sen, B. 42
senior administrators 10, 90, 91
sensitivity analysis 45
service provision, rural 33
settlement requirements 78
Shaner, W.W. 67

Shore, A.R. 36, 63
showpiece villages 55
Simmonds, E. 67, 70
Simmonds, N.W.
slavery 38, 86
smallholder 68, 69
Smith, N.L. 26
Smith, W.
social forestry 26, 96
soft models 68
soft science 68
Somalia 34
sondeo 61, 71, 72
Southeast Asia 39
Spanish Basque town 60
spheres of activity v, vi, vii, 2, 9, 12, 13, 74
stage-managed visits 57
statistics 1, 23, 24, 48
statistical analysis 1, 24
statistical confidence 23
statistical inferences 48
Stephens, D. 47
Stewart, I. 45
Stonecash, J. 19
Strauss, A.L. 3, 36
Streiffeler, F. 3
subjective ranking 42
successive approximation approach 61
Sudan 86
Sukumaland 72
Sutherland, A. 38, 73
Tanzania 33, 72, 78
tapes 53
task variation 27
team studies v, 54, 61
technical services 2
technology development vi, 3, 13, 67, 68, 74
technology screening 16
Thailand 39
theology 36
theoretical physics 36
Therkildsen, O. 33
Third World 44, 47, 96
Thoolen, B. 26
Thrupp, L.A. 68, 73
time-horizons 74
TOT see: transfer of technology
trade credit 49
traders 41, 50, 81, 80-82
training vi, 3, 7, 14, 17, 28, 40, 60, 61, 63, 87, 89, 90, 92

transdisciplinary 54
transfer of technology vi, 67, 68, 69
transport 11, 19, 22, 27-29, 52, 78, 80, 85
trend, M.G. 47, 48, 86
triangulation v, vii, 2, 46-49, 51, 60, 90
Tripp, R. 73
Trow, M. 46
United Kingdom iv, 60
United Nations 8
university 39, 90
UNRISD 8
Uphoff, N. 43, 74, 75
urban, L.V. 55
urbanization 30
United States Agency for International Development 39, 41, 70, 75
Van Maanen, J. 36
villagization 78
Vulliamy, G. 38, 47
Washington 65
water development 26
water supply 11, 31, 33
Water Supply Board 33

wealth ranking vii, 40, 84, 89
welfare 8, 11, 41
Wellard, K. 62
Wengle, J.L. 36
White, L.G. 18, 44, 77, 96
Whiteford, S. 44
Whyte, A.V. 36
Whyte, W.F. 46
Wiggins, S. 21
Wilson, F. 34
Wilson, K. 68-70
Wolcott, H.F. 37
Wood, G.D. 62
World Bank 1, 17, 20, 23, 26, 34, 45, 54, 60
Wotowiec, P. Jr 73
yam vii, 59
Year of the Woman 56
yields per hectare 16, 64
Yin, R.K. 73
Young, F.W. 11, 65, 64, 74, 82, 85, 96
Young, R.A.
Zandstra, H. 38, 71
Zimbabwe 57